K

Time

Prime Time

A History of the Middle Aged in Twentieth-century Britain

JOHN BENSON

Longman
London and New York

Addison Wesley Longman Limited
Edinburgh Gate
Harlow
Essex CM20 2JE
United Kingdom
and Associated Companies throughout the world

*Published in the United States of America
by Addison Wesley Longman Inc., New York*

First published 1997

ISBN 0 582 25658 5 CSD
0 582 25657 7 PPR

British Library Cataloguing-in-Publication Data

A catalogue record for this book is available from the British Library

Library of Congress Cataloging-in-Publication Data

Benson, John, 1945–
Prime time : a history of the middle aged in twentieth-century Britain / John
Benson.
p. cm.
Includes bibliographical references and index.
ISBN 0–582–25658–5 (CSD). — ISBN 0–582–25657–7 (PPR)
1. Middle age—Great Britain—History—20th century. 2. Middle
aged persons—Great Britain—History—20th century. I. Title.
HQ1059.5.G7B46 1997
305.244′0941′0904—dc21   97–20597
                                                                CIP

Set by 35 in 10/12pt Baskerville
Produced by Longman Singapore Publishers (Pte) Ltd.
Printed in Singapore

Contents

List of Figures

Acknowledgements

I know a good deal about middle age. I started this book when I was 48, and finished it when I was 51. When I was 48 I celebrated my silver wedding anniversary, when I was 49 I was told that I might have glaucoma, when I was 50 I received birthday cards saying that although I didn't look fifty I probably had done once, and when I was 51 my wife and I decided to try to save seriously for retirement.

Fortunately, the temptation to pontificate on the basis of my own experience has been tempered by the information, advice and criticism which I have received from the friends, colleagues and scholars with whom I have discussed my work. I have benefited from the opportunity to present my arguments to a number of different audiences: the department of history colloquium, University of Calgary; the department of philosophy, history and politics colloquium, University College of the Cariboo; the MA in the history of the Manchester region day school, Manchester Metropolitan University; the postgraduate seminar, history department, University of Southampton; the history research seminar, University of Wolverhampton; the conference on 'Aspects of the history of the British middle class c. 1700 to the present' at Manchester Metropolitan University; and the Social History Society conference on 'The social history of the workplace' at the University of Strathclyde.

I have also benefited from the interest and assistance of Tom Almond, Bernice Andrews, Alan Apperley, Paula Bartley, Jon Bernades, Nick Birch, Kenneth D. Brown, Wiz Cameron, Nancy Cox, David Denham, Martin Durham, Frank Eves, Diana Holmes, Roger Leese, Elizabeth Roberts, Roger Seddon, Peter Urwin, Peter Watson and Harvey Woolf. I have benefited in particular from the encouragement and generosity of those who have worked more closely with me. Andrew MacLennan continued to combine enthusiasm, caution and criticism in just the right proportions; Christopher Bennett and Steven Nicholls provided valuable research assistance; Richard Sykes prepared the figures; Helen Jones helped to improve chapter 3; while Lorraine Boul, Mike Hepworth, Geoff Hurd and

Julie Skucha generously took time from their own work to read and discuss a draft of the entire manuscript. However, my greatest debt is once again to Clare Benson who provided support, encouragement and a great deal more.

John Benson
November 1996

CHAPTER ONE

Introduction

The history of age and ageing has received increasing attention in recent years. Psychologists, economists, sociologists, gerontologists, geographers and historians have all begun to recognise that age (along with gender, race, region, religion and class) could – and often did – constitute a crucial determinant of economic, social and cultural life.[1]

However, such recognition remains remarkably limited and unbalanced. Those concerned with the effects of age and ageing continue to concentrate their attention upon just three stages of the life cycle: childhood, adolescence and old age. There has been a long-standing, though often sentimental and rather Whiggish concern with the nation's children: the ways in which they were brought up, the work that they were expected to do, and the relationships that they formed with parents, teachers, employers and the wider world.[2] This interest has been supplemented since the 1960s by a desire to understand the history of adolescence: the clothes that young people wore, the music that they listened to and the

1. See, for example, A. S. Rossi, 'Life-span Theories and Women's Lives', *Signs: Journal of Women in Culture and Society*, 6, 1980; M. Anderson, 'The Emergence of the Modern Life Cycle in Britain', *Social History*, 10, 1985; T. K. Hareven and K. J. Adams (eds), *Ageing and Life Course Transitions: An Interdisciplinary Perspective*, Tavistock, 1992; J. Bond and P. Coleman (eds), *Ageing in Society: An Introduction to Social Gerontology*, Sage, 1990. Place of publication is London unless otherwise stated.
2. For recent studies, see P. Horn, *Children's Work and Welfare, 1780–1880*, Macmillan, Basingstoke, 1994; E. Hopkins, *Childhood Transformed: Working-class Children in Nineteenth-century England*, Manchester University Press, Manchester, 1994; P. Bolin-Hort, *Work, Family and the State: Child Labour and the Organisation of Production in the British Cotton Industry, 1780–1920*, Lund University Press, Lund, 1989; S. Humphries, *Hooligans or Rebels? An Oral History of Working-class Childhood 1889–1939*, Blackwell, Oxford, 1981.

threat, whether real or imagined, that they posed to the existing
social order.[3]

In more recent years, these interests have been supplemented –
one is tempted to say replaced – by a powerful and rapidly growing
preoccupation with the history of old age. For the past and the
present are more intimately entwined than many imagine, and our
generation, like those before it, tends to interpret the past in the
light of its own experiences, interests and anxieties. It is no co-
incidence therefore that as it has begun to dawn upon us that the
ageing of the late twentieth-century population threatens to create
a so-called demographic time bomb, historians have redoubled their
efforts to understand the lives of the elderly in earlier generations
and earlier centuries.[4]

Yet even those most concerned with the history of age and ageing
have displayed surprisingly little interest in the history of middle age.[5]
It is true, of course, that a good deal of history is by the middle
aged, about the middle aged, for the middle aged. It is the middle
aged, after all, who make up the bulk of professional historians, it
is the middle aged about whom most history is written – and it is
the middle aged who provide the norms and values against which
other groups seek to assert their separate identities. The trouble is
that such perspectives and preoccupations have rarely been recognised, made explicit and subjected to the careful scrutiny which
they deserve.

3. I. K. Ben-Amos, *Adolescence and Youth in Early Modern England*, Yale University
Press, New Haven, CT, 1994; G. Pearson, *Hooligan: A History of Respectable Fears*,
Macmillan, Basingstoke, 1983; H. Hendrick, *Images of Youth: Age, Class and the Male
Youth Problem, 1880–1920*, Clarendon Press, Oxford, 1990; D. Fowler, 'Teenage Con-
sumers? Young Wage-earners and Leisure in Manchester, 1919–1939', in A. Davies
and S. Fielding (eds), *Workers' Worlds: Cultures and Communities in Manchester and
Salford, 1880–1939*, Manchester University Press, Manchester, 1992; S. Hall and
T. Jefferson (eds), *Resistance through Rituals: Youth Sub-cultures in Post-war Britain*,
Hutchinson, 1976.
4. General studies include P. Laslett, 'The History of Ageing and the Aged', in V.
Carver and P. Liddiard (eds), *An Ageing Population: A Reader and Sourcebook*, Hodder
and Stoughton, 1978; D. Eversley, 'Some New Aspects of Ageing in Britain', in
Hareven and Adams, *Ageing*; P. Johnson, 'Old Age and Ageing in Britain', *ReFresh*,
17, 1993. For more specialised studies, see C. Phillipson, *Capitalism and the Construction of Old Age*, Macmillan, Basingstoke, 1982; L. Hannah, *Inventing Retirement: The
Development of Occupational Pensions in Britain*, Cambridge University Press, Cambridge,
1986; P. Johnson, 'The Employment and Retirement of Older Men in England
and Wales, 1881–1981', *Economic History Review*, xlvii, 1994.
5. There exists, of course, a long tradition of literary interest in middle age. See,
for example, W. Somerset Maugham, *The Moon and Sixpence*, Heinemann, 1919; A.
Wilson, *The Middle Age of Mrs Eliot*, Secker and Warburg, 1958; G. Orwell, *Coming Up
for Air*, Penguin, 1962; M. Drabble, *A Natural Curiosity*, Viking, 1989; D. Lodge,
Therapy, Secker and Warburg, 1993; M. Gee, *Lost Children*, Flamingo, 1995.

It is also the case that there have been a large number of self-help guides designed to ease middle-class readers through the anxieties of their middle years.[6] It is true, finally, that the ageing of the generation born immediately after the Second World War has provided journalists, commentators and other pundits with countless opportunities to discuss the perils, pitfalls and possibilities of middle-aged life. In the mid 1990s, for example, they marvelled as the Rolling Stones turned fifty, mocked the middle-aged indiscretions of public figures like Phil Collins and Hartley Booth, revelled gleefully in Janet Street-Porter's broadside on television executives for being male, middle-class, middle-brow and middle-aged, and worried increasingly about 'how to survive something more devastating than drink, drugs and divorce': middle age.[7]

The ageing of the post-war generation has produced other, more substantial contributions. In 1991, fifty-two-year-old Germaine Greer published her best-selling study, *The Change: Women, Ageing and the Menopause*, a book that was designed, *inter alia*, to attack hormone replacement therapy and suggest 'role models for the ageing woman, role models who are not simply glittering threads, some bones, some silastic and hanks of hand-knotted bought hair'.[8] Three years later, fifty-two-year-old Erica Yong produced an autobiographical volume entitled *Fear of Fifty: A Midlife Memoir*. Looking back on the first fifty years of her life, she described herself as a woman of the 'whiplash generation', 'a generation reared to be Doris Day, coming of age wanting to be Gloria Steinem, and bringing up daughters in the age of Princess Di and Madonna'.[9]

6. For example, S. Taylor, *Health for the Middle Aged*, Methuen, 1915; A. Lorand, *Old Age Deferred: The Causes of Old Age and Its Postponement by Hygienic and Therapeutic Measures*, Davis, Philadelphia 1922; L. Williams, *Middle Age and Old Age*, Oxford University Press, Oxford, 1925; E. L. Hopeworth-Ash, *On Middle-age and Keeping Young*, Mills and Boon, 1927; S. Trent, *Women Over Forty*, Duckworth, 1935; M. C. Stopes, *Change of Life in Men and Women*, Putnam, 1936; The Amalgamated Press Ltd., *Every Woman's Guide of Love & Marriage and Family Life*, Amalgamated Press, n.d.; A. Torrie, *The Middle-aged Man: The Way of Understanding*, Church Information Office, 1959; A Country Doctor, *Facing Retirement: A Guide for the Middle-aged and Elderly*, Allen and Unwin, 1960; J. Malleson, *Facts and Fallacies of Middle Age*, Penguin, 1963; Consumers' Association, *Living Through Middle Age*, Consumers' Association, 1976; M. Fiske, *Middle Age: The Prime of Life?*, Harper & Row, New York, c. 1070.

7. *Sunday Times*, 11 September 1994; *The Times*, 26 August 1995; *Guardian*, 8 January 1996; 'Baby Boomers on a Spending Spree', *Independent*, 10 January 1996; 'My Geriatric Generation', *Guardian*, 9 July 1996.

8. G. Greer, *The Change: Women, Ageing and the Menopause*, Penguin, 1992, p. 8.

9. E. Yong, *Fear of Fifty: A Midlife Memoir*, Chatto & Windus, 1994, dust cover. Also B. Friedan, *The Fountain of Age*, Vintage, 1994.

The academic community has been slow to respond to such promptings. The few scholarly books dealing with middle age were mostly written some time ago, dealt primarily with the United States of America, and were written by (and for) psychiatrists, social workers and health-care professionals.[10] In Great Britain, the history of middle age has attracted the serious attention of only two scholars, Mike Featherstone and Mike Hepworth, who during the 1980s produced a series of pioneering and often fascinating sociological-cum-historical studies of issues such as the meaning of middle age, attitudes towards those in their middle years, and the history of the male menopause.[11]

Accordingly, it is the purpose of this book to rescue the history of middle age from the deadly combination of neglect and condescension with which it has been treated. However, this is, of necessity, a partial and preliminary study. There is nothing here about those from ethnic, sexual and other minorities; there is virtually nothing about the public policy implications of middle age, and there is less than there should be about the experiences of those who were middle-aged in Wales, Scotland and the English regions.

The focus here is upon the complex, and contradictory, relationship between representation and reality. The book aims to explore the disjuncture that developed between the growing demonisation of middle age and the improvements that occurred in the day-to-day lives of those in their forties and fifties. It aims, more specifically, to examine the ways in which middle age has been defined, the health that the middle aged enjoyed, the material circumstances in which they found themselves, the relationships which they formed with their families, and the ways in which they looked at the world round about them. Why, it will be asked, has middle age received such a bad press? Is it true that middle age is – and always has been – a time of physical decline and emotional instability? Is it

10. For example, K. Soddy and M. Kidson, *Men in Middle Life*, Lippincott, 1967; B. L. Neugarten (ed.), *Middle Age and Aging: A Reader in Social Psychology*, University of Chicago Press, Chicago, IL, 1968; W. H. Norman and T. J. Scarmella (eds), *Midlife: Developmental and Clinical Issues*, Brunner/Mazel, New York 1980. But see R. Bell (ed.), *Middle Age*, BBC, 1967; G. Sheehy, *Passages: Predictable Crises of Adult Life*, Dutton, Harmondsworth 1974.

11. M. Hepworth and M. Featherstone, *Surviving Middle Age*, Blackwell, Oxford, 1982; M. Featherstone and M. Hepworth, 'Changing Images of Middle Age', in M. L. Johnson (ed.), *Transitions in Middle and Later Life*, British Society of Gerontology, 1980; M. Featherstone and M. Hepworth, 'Aging and Inequality: Consumer Culture and the New Middle Age', in D. Robbins (ed.), *Rethinking Social Inequality*, Gower, Aldershot, 1982; M. Featherstone and M. Hepworth, 'The History of the Male Menopause 1848–1936', *Maturitas*, 7, 1985; M. Hepworth, 'The Mid Life Phase', in G. Cohen (ed.), *Social Change and the Life Course*, Tavistock, 1987.

fair to categorise the middle aged as rigid, judgemental and set in their ways?

Of course, such questions are a good deal easier to ask than they are to answer. Indeed, it is important to appreciate that many of the arguments being propounded, particularly towards the end of the book, should be treated less as conclusions to be accepted than as propositions to be tested. Nonetheless, it is believed that significant progress has been made towards beginning to unravel the history of middle age during the course of the twentieth century.

It will be shown first that there developed a growing divergence between the representation and the reality of middle age; that although middle age became regarded as increasingly undesirable, the lives of the middle aged became increasingly healthy, prosperous and enjoyable. Secondly, it will be suggested that this health, prosperity and enjoyment depended less upon attitude, choice and lifestyle than upon biology, gender and class: the middle aged, it seems, were less likely to experience the middle age to which they aspired than the middle age to which their circumstances predisposed them. Thirdly, it will be argued that middle age – and age more generally – constitutes an important category for historical analysis, a category which, like gender, race, region, religion and class, should inform any attempt to understand the society in which we live. It is hoped therefore that this book will prove of interest not just to those concerned for personal reasons with the onset of middle age but to all those wishing to disentangle the complex economic, social and cultural history of twentieth-century Britain.

CHAPTER TWO

Meanings and Numbers

There has never been any agreement as to the meaning of middle age, and any agreement therefore as to the number, and proportion, of the population that should be described as middle-aged. Nor is this at all surprising. For ageing, it has been pointed out, 'is the most idiosyncratic of all human processes and predictions cannot be made about any individual's ageing career'.[1] Moreover, middle age is among the most difficult of all ages to define satisfactorily. For middle age, unlike childhood and old age, does not even have a fixed start point (birth) or end point (death) to provide the basis from which to build a definition likely to acquire general acceptance.[2]

Thus middle age has been defined in several contrasting – and often contradictory – ways. Some commentators defined it biologically, as the period during which certain physical and physiological changes occurred. These were the years, it was suggested, during which the body began to let one down: women underwent the menopause and men started to have problems with the prostate.[3] Others defined it psychologically and socially, as the years during which the attitudes of those experiencing – and observing – such changes began to alter. 'Sooner or later the middle-aged woman becomes aware of a change in the attitude of other people towards her. She can no longer trade on her appearance.'[4] Others commentators again

1. G. Greer, *The Change: Women, Ageing and the Menopause*, Penguin, 1992, p. 5.
2. F. Bell, 'On Some Difficulties Incidental to Middle Age', *The Nineteenth Century*, March 1900, p. 459; D. B. Bromley, 'Middle Age: An Introduction', in R. Bell (ed.), *Middle Age*, BBC, 1967, pp. 7–8; J. Roebuck, 'When Does Old Age Begin?: The Evolution of the English Definition', *Journal of Social History*, 12, 1979, p. 416.
3. R. Briggs, 'Biological Ageing', in J. Bond and P. Coleman (eds), *Ageing in Society: An Introduction to Social Gerontology*, Sage, 1990.
4. Greer, *The Change*, pp. 6–7.

defined middle age in chronological terms. Middle age occurred, it was said, between certain fixed points: between the ages of thirty and fifty,[5] thirty and fifty-five,[6] thirty-five and fifty,[7] forty and fifty-five,[8] forty and sixty,[9] forty-five and fifty-five,[10] forty-five and sixty-four[11] or, most peculiarly, between forty-nine and sixty-three.[12]

Yet this is not the end of the matter. For middle age has been defined differently for men and women, and differently too for the middle class and working class. Men, it was often assumed, aged later – and better – than women.[13] 'Thus, for most women, aging means a humiliating process of gradual sexual disqualification. Since women are considered maximally eligible in early youth, after which their sexual value drops steadily, even young women feel themselves in a desperate race against the calendar.'[14] Nor was this necessarily the crude sexism that it appears at first sight. For as Tamara Hareven points out, it cannot be assumed that 'people of identical age share the same experiences or move through the same aging process': 'men and women of the same age will have had very dissimilar pasts, strikingly different ongoing experiences, and largely divergent developmental futures'.[15]

Middle age has also been defined differently for the middle class and working class. The middle class, it was often suggested, aged later – and better – than the working class. 'Poor people look old much earlier in their lives than do rich people. But anxiety about aging is certainly more common, and more acute, among

5. *Census of Great Britain*, 1851, *Report*, p. ix; *Mass-Observation's Weekly*, 21 June 1943.

6. A. Collin, 'Mid-career Change: An Exploratory Study of the Process of "Career" and of the Experience of Change in "Mid Life"', PhD University of Loughborough, 1984.

7. 'Active 54' to *Lancet*, 5 September 1914.

8. *British Medical Journal*, 1 August 1964.

9. *British Medical Journal*, 10 July 1915; B. Friedan, *The Fountain of Age*, Vintage, 1994, p. 29.

10. Greer, *The Change*, p. 26.

11. *Report of the Committee on the Economic and Financial Problems of the Provision for Old Age*, 1954, Appendix.

12. *British Medical Journal*, 10 July 1915. According to a National Opinion Poll carried out in 1988, people's definition of middle age depended upon their age. *Weekend*, 15 October 1988.

13. L. Fairfield, 'An Address on the Health of Professional Women', *Lancet*, 3 July 1926; *Woman's Journal*, October, November 1933; *Woman*, 13 February 1960; J. Jakeman, 'Mutton Dressed as Ram', *Guardian*, 2 October 1995.

14. S. Sontag, 'The Double Standard of Ageing', in V. Carver and P. Liddiard (eds), *An Ageing Population: A Reader and Sourcebook*, Hodder and Stoughton, 1978, p. 75. Also Bell, 'Difficulties', p. 469; Friedan, *Fountain of Age*, pp. 113, 336.

15. T. K. Hareven, 'Historical Perspectives', in T. K. Hareven and K. J. Adams (eds), *Ageing and Life Course Transitions: An Interdisciplinary Perspective*, Tavistock, 1982, p. 63.

middle-class and rich women than among working-class women.'[16] Again this is not a view that can simply be dismissed out of hand. For as Hareven points out, 'we know that a cohort may be deeply divided by the economic [and social] conditions its members have experienced and that these divisions have a remarkable tenacity through the life course'.[17]

Accordingly, this chapter has three broad, and deceptively simple, objectives: to examine the ways in which the meaning of middle age has changed over time; to provide a working definition of middle age; and to use this definition to calculate the number, and proportion, of the population that should be described as middle-aged at various points over the past hundred years. It will be argued that the meaning of middle age has changed in several significant respects, and that the number, and proportion, of the population that should be described as middle-aged has grown substantially since the beginning of the twentieth century.

The meaning of middle age (and its derivatives middle-aged, middle-ageing and so on) has changed, and changed significantly, during the course of the twentieth century. There have been three major developments: middle age became defined increasingly often in chronological terms; became associated unambiguously with decay and collapse; but came to be regarded as largely, if not completely avoidable given the appropriate remedial action.[18]

Chronological definitions of middle age

There is no doubt that middle age became defined increased commonly in chronological terms. For although middle age continued to be understood biologically, psychologically and socially,[19] it was the chronological definition that was to assume prominence. Indeed, as time went by, middle age was defined with increasing chronological

16. Sontag, 'Double Standard', p. 76. Also *Daily Mail*, 5 January 1925; W. Gordon, 'The Life-style of the Affluent Middle Aged', *ADMAP*, February 1981, p. 72.
17. Hareven, 'Historical Perspectives', p. 63. Also Roebuck, 'Old Age', p. 418.
18. M. Featherstone and M. Hepworth, 'Changing Images of Middle Age', in M. L. Johnson (ed.), *Transitions in Middle and Later Life*, British Society of Gerontology, 1980.
19. *Daily Mail*, 4 January, 9 September 1905, 31 August 1915, 2 January 1925, 3 January 1935, 5 September 1955; *Woman's Own*, 30 October 1915; *The Rayoneer*, January 1934; *News of the World*, 4 June 1995; M. Hepworth and M. Featherstone, *Surviving Middle Age*, Blackwell, Oxford, 1982, ch. 1.

precision: middle age, it came to be accepted, began at forty and ended some time around the age of sixty.

The years selected to represent middle age changed, as one might expect, according to changing economic, social and demographic circumstances.[20] During the second half of the nineteenth century, when average life expectancy stood at less than fifty, those responsible for the compilation of the census felt confident that middle age could be defined, for both men and women, as the period that fell between the ages of thirty and fifty.[21]

Those living in the early twentieth century felt, not surprisingly, that middle age began somewhat later. With life expectancy rising nearly 30 per cent between 1901 and 1931, many came to believe that middle age started, not at thirty, but at thirty-five.[22] In 1914 a correspondent calling himself 'Active 54' wrote to the *Lancet* to discuss middle age, 'the period ... that lies between 35 and 50 years'.[23] Advertisers and journalists too began to accept that thirty-five, rather than thirty, marked the onset of middle age. It was claimed in the early 1930s, for instance, that de Kuyper's Hollands tonic provided 'a safe and splendid aid to the middle aged': it was a product, it was promised, which will 'help you over the difficult years' between thirty-five and forty-five.[24] Forty years later, the *Daily Sketch* remarked that 'Elvis Presley becomes officially middle-aged on Thursday. It marks his 35th birthday.'[25] In fact, by the end of the century some had come to believe that it was forty-five or fifty that marked the decisive turning point, with one 1980s acronym – TOAFF – referring to those who were 'too old at forty-five'.[26]

However, forty it was that came to be regarded as marking the onset of middle age. For as the *Lancet* explained in 1920, forty fell 'half-way through what we all hope may be our span of life'.[27] Newspapers began to carry articles comparing the years 'before and

20. *British Medical Journal*, 10 July 1915.

21. *Census of Great Britain*, 1851, *Report*, p. ix; *Census of England and Wales*, 1871, *General Report*, p. xii.

22. H. Jones, *Health and Society in Twentieth-century Britain*, Longman, 1994, p. 196. Also *Family Doctor*, 22 October 1910; *Sunday Graphic*, 9 August 1931.

23. 'Active 54' to *Lancet*, 5 September 1914.

24. *Woman's Journal*, October 1993. Also *Daily Sketch*, 2 February 1959.

25. *Daily Sketch*, 6 January 1970. Also Evelyn Home in *Woman*, 4 March 1950; Maurice Wiggins in *Sunday Graphic*, 5 February 1950.

26. *Weekend*, 3 December 1988. Also A Country Doctor, *Facing Retirement: A Guide for the Middle Aged and Elderly*, Allen and Unwin, 1960; Gordon, 'Life-style', p. 72.

27. *Lancet*, 1 May 1920. Also 14 September 1907, 26 July 1930, 23 October 1943; 'AETAS' to *British Medical Journal*, 12 February 1921; *Woman's Own*, 3 July 1915.

after forty',[28] discussing 'the nightmare birthday' – forty of course[29] – and investigating what they liked to describe as the 'dangerous forties'. Middle age, it was explained in the 1940s, was like the middle five miles of a fifteen mile journey: it was the stretch 'where so many stop and give up'.[30] Middle age, it was reported in 1985, was a time that some tried to mark in ambitious and ingenious ways.

> A Huddersfield accountant, John Lamb, provided 40 friends with a warm way to celebrate his 40th birthday. They arrived at a tennis court at 6 a.m. and told to prepare for a warm weekend, whereupon they were taken for a four day break – Majorca.[31]

Indeed, it is striking that from the 1930s onwards advertisers began to draw upon, develop, and no doubt reinforce, the popular impression that forty marked the onset of middle age. Products like Phyllosan were aimed specifically at the middle aged. 'A woman of forty is at the crossroads of life', it was pointed out in 1938, 'Continued youthfulness and vitality lie one way, premature old age the other.'[32] By the 1960s, high-protein breakfast cereals such as Special K were described as ideal both for young mothers and for the over-forties who 'need protein to help maintain and repair tissues'.[33] In fact, by the 1980s and 1990s, those turning forty could expect to receive gifts of Phyllosan, special commercially produced greeting cards and, if they were unlucky, to find photographs of themselves as children peering out from the classified columns of their local newspaper.[34]

It is striking too that even those wishing to suggest that middle age began at some other age, felt compelled to acknowledge, and challenge, the popular impression that it was forty that marked the crucial turning point. As a reviewer in the *British Medical Journal* argued in 1915, 'Taking into consideration the changed conditions of modern life, and the improved facilities for postponing the onset of senility', forty-nine rather than forty should mark the beginning of middle age.[35] Such comparisons became more and more common. In 1950, a correspondent to *John Bull* maintained that

28. *Sunday Graphic*, 7 July 1935.
29. *John Bull*, 14 June 1930. Also *Weekend*, 24 September 1988.
30. Rev. W. H. Elliott in *Sunday Graphic*, 22 February 1948.
31. *Daily Mail*, 12 January 1985.
32. *Woman*, 2 April 1938. Also 19 March 1938, 23 March 1940; *John Bull*, 15 March 1930; *Woman's Way*, 26 January 1935; *Sun*, 5, 19 October 1966.
33. *Woman*, 2 April 1960.
34. Wolverhampton Oral History Project (hereafter WOH), Mr F.
35. *British Medical Journal*, 10 July 1915.

'While it is true that people are living longer, it also certain that they retain their youth much longer. A woman at forty is not middle-aged now as she was in Victorian times.'[36] There can be little doubt then that by the middle of the century, the idea that middle age began at forty had taken deep root in the national consciousness.[37]

There was never nearly as much interest in when it was that middle age ended. However, there was considerable interest – though this was not quite the same thing – in when it was that old age began.[38] Some commentators believed it started at fifty-five, others at sixty, others at fifty-five for men and sixty for women, and other again at sixty for men and sixty-five for women. As the *Family Doctor* explained rather confusingly in 1890, 'the period of incipient old age is usually fixed in women about the fifty-third, in men about the sixtieth year'.[39] It was a confusion that was never quite resolved.[40] Nonetheless, as Janet Roebuck points out, a working definition did emerge: 'the sociologists, behavioural scientists, and other investigators involved in the study of [the] aged have tended, as has 20th century society in general, to accept the government's "pension age" or "retirement age" as the convenient dividing line between mature adulthood and old age.'[41]

It was generally accepted therefore that middle age could, and should, be defined with chronological precision. 'What, precisely, is middle age?' demanded a doctor in 1915. 'Most people, perhaps, would say in two decades – between 40 and 60.'[42] It was an answer with which more and more of the population were likely to agree as the century wore on. Middle age occurred, it came to be accepted, between the ages of forty and sixty.

Such chronological precision was accompanied by, and coalesced with, a convergence in popular attitudes towards the middle aged. For whereas ideas about middle age had been divided sharply along gender and class lines during the second half of the nineteenth

36. E. Buss to *John Bull*, 11 March 1950.

37. See, for example, *Sunday Graphic*, 5 February 1950. Also *Tit-Bits*, 16, 23 January 1965; *Weekend*, 15 October, 29 October, 5 November 1988.

38. C. Phillipson, *Capitalism and the Construction of Old Age*, Macmillan, Basingstoke, 1982.

39. *Family Doctor*, 15 February 1890. Cf. *Report of the Royal Commission on the Aged Poor*, II, 1895, Q. 2,002–5, J. H. Allen.

40. See, for example, *British Medical Journal*, 19 January 1907; Greer, *The Change*, p. 26.

41. Roebuck, 'Old Age', p. 417. Also *British Medical Journal*, 21 September 1957; Friedan, *Fountain of Age*, p. 567. Cf. *R. C. Economic Problems*, p. 49; *National Advisory Committee on the Employment of Older Men and Women, First Report*, 1953, p. 81.

42. *British Medical Journal*, 10 July 1915.

century, they began to converge significantly during the course of the twentieth century. The middle aged, whether male or female, middle-class or working-class, became associated more and more with a broadly similar set of physical failings and psychological difficulties.

Demonisation

Middle age became associated unambiguously with decay and collapse. The sharp distinction that late nineteenth- and early twentieth-century commentators had drawn between men's and women's experience of middle age began to diminish. Of course, women continued to be stigmatised. In fact, describing a woman as middle-aged remained a convenient, short-hand way of depicting her as fat, frumpy, bossy, emotional, irrational and impossible to deal with.[43] 'It was inevitable', it was explained in 1969, 'that students would eventually come to revolt against the menopausal leadership of the NUS and its flaccid policies.'[44] 'How would you feel', Michael Parkinson asked a radio audience in 1994, if a 'batty, middle-aged woman ran into your kitchen and started throwing spinach around?'[45] Shoplifters, many people believed, were most often women: either a 'menopausal lady, ancient widow or divorcee'.[46]

The reason for such behaviour – or rather for such assumptions – lay, of course, in popular beliefs about the menopause. As Marie Stopes argued in 1936, 'The "difficulties" of the menopause in women are chiefly the physical expression of mental states induced by fears of all the falsities and hoodoos put into circulation by rumour.'[47] Yet such fears did not owe their existence entirely to rumour and innuendo. Self-help guides and medical opinion no doubt played a part too in the propagation of popular ideas about what it was to be a middle-aged woman. *Every Woman's Book of Love & Marriage and Family Life* began its chapter on 'Married Life in the

43. *Daily Mail*, 3 May 1960; Greer, *The Change*, p. 336; A. Sharman, *The Middle Years: The Change of Life*, Livingstone, 1962, introduction; J. Le Carré, *The Night Manager*, Coronet, 1994, p. 35.
44. J. A. Simpson and E. S. C. Weiner (eds), *The Oxford English Dictionary*, Clarendon Press, Oxford, 1989 (hereafter OED), IX, p. 743. Also *Daily Mail*, 3 May 1960.
45. *Guardian*, 11 May 1994.
46. R. Davey, 'Shoplifting: How Much Do We Really Know?', *Retail & Distribution Management*, 5, 1977, p. 7.
47. M. C. Stopes, *Change of Life in Men and Women*, Pitman, 1936, p. 11. Also Greer, *The Change*, p. 77.

Forties' with the words: 'Middle age has its own special physical and mental problems for all married people. In the case of women a stage is gradually reached which is often called the "Change of Life" and which is finally marked by the ceasing to function of the sexual organs.'[48] An editorial in the *Lancet* explained in 1975 that the menopause meant temporary problems like hot flushes, long-term difficulties such as cancer and osteoporosis, and 'perhaps most important of all, the loss of femininity associated with progressive atrophy of the secondary sexual characteristics'.[49] The Consumers' Association's guide to *Living Through Middle Age*, which was published in the following year, encapsulated prevailing views about the relationship between the menopause, attitudes and behaviour. 'At the menopause, irritability tends to be a problem, and is similar to (and probably has similar biochemical causes as) premenstrual tension.'

> Tension may lead to poor concentration and memory lapses. Or it may make a woman feel that she is going out of her mind. Mood changes include anxiety, depression, apathy or inertia, lethargy, feelings of being inadequate or worthless, occasionally of persecution when she feels that everyone is against her and trivialities may be magnified and lead to brooding and complaints.[50]

Homogenisation

However, as time went by women became unable to lay exclusive claim even to the menopause. There were a growing number of commentators who, while accepting the existence of the menopause, claimed that it did not widen the gap between men and women in the way, and to the extent, that was usually suggested. The midlife crisis was felt increasingly to crush both men and women, involving the middle aged of both sexes in anxiety about their physical failings, their deteriorating appearance, the years they had wasted and the old age and death that lay ahead of them.

The view that men underwent their own version of the menopause has a surprisingly long history. The book *What a Woman of*

48. The Amalgamated Press Ltd., *Every Woman's Book of Love & Marriage and Family Life*, Amalgamated Press, n.d., p. 162.

49. *Lancet*, 7 June 1975.

50. Consumers' Association, *Living Through Middle Age*, Consumers' Association, 1976, p. 81.

Forty-Five Ought to Know was published in 1902, and contained a short chapter entitled 'The Wife's Duty To Her Husband'.

> She must remember that he too has come to a time of life when he has not quite the mental and physical poise he once had, and that patience is as much a cardinal virtue in the wife towards her husband, at this time, as in the husband towards the wife.[51]

The early 1930s saw renewed claims that the menopuase 'was a condition common to both sexes'.[52] In general, reported one medical expert, 'the mental and physical changes at the climacteric are of the same order in men as women'.[53] Nearly fifty years later, the Consumers' Association remained broadly in agreement.

> A man who has had difficulties in adapting to the stressful periods of puberty, adolescence, marriage, parenthood, and who has been unable to deal successfully with anxieties and guilt, is predisposed to go through a psychologically disturbing period with perhaps sexual difficulties in middle age.[54]

Some commentators went further still. In 1994 the *Guardian* carried a lengthy article entitled 'The Men in Menopause'. Its message could scarcely have been clearer.

> the ageing process is genderless; as unspeakably vile for men as for women. Men do not have menses to pause or cycles to interrupt when they reach the stage of life when intimations of mortality are not just misfortunes that strike other people. But they do sweat. They do lose their beauty. They do suffer the damnably humiliating side-effects of menopause: the depression, the fatigue, despair, irritability, shame, panic and loss of libido.[55]

The clear distinction that late nineteenth-century commentators had drawn between the middle-class and working-class experience of middle age also began to break down. This is not to deny, of course, that popular views about the nature of ageing continued to display some recognition of the role that class might play. The middle age of middle-class men continued to be associated, to some

---

51. M. Featherstone and M. Hepworth, 'The History of the Male Menopause 1848–1936', *Maturitas*, 7, 1985, pp. 252–3. Also Featherstone and Hepworth, *Surviving Middle Age*, pp. 29–39.
52. *Lancet*, 11 October 1930. Also 13 December 1930.
53. *British Medical Journal*, 13 December 1930. Also Stopes, *Change of Life*, ch. 3; *Every Woman's Book*, pp. 167–9.
54. Consumers' Association, *Middle Age*, p. 108. Also *OED*, IX, p. 607.
55. *Guardian Weekend*, 23 April 1994. Also A. Ferriman, 'The Prime of Life, or the Time of Life?', *Independent on Sunday*, 4 June 1995.

extent at least, with maturity, stability and wisdom; the middle age of working-class men with incapacity, instability and decline.

Such distinctions were drawn particularly vividly around the turn of the century. For as the *Family Doctor* explained in 1890, hair – or the lack of it – served as a powerful signifier of the advantages of middle-class ageing. 'It is, no doubt, very much to the advantage of a young practitioner to exhibit a modern antique appearance, and nothing contributes so greatly to this end as a head which is innocent of hair.'[56] Twenty years later, the journal discussed more fully what it saw as the advantages of middle-class ageing and the disadvantages of working-class ageing.

> Practically, no British statesmen of the highest rank are under forty, most of them are above fifty, and often ten years older than that. In the trades, on the other hand, the highest paid workmen, with hardly an exception, are under the age of two score.[57]

Such distinctions began to break down, with popular ideas about middle age converging substantially during the course of the twentieth century. There were two distinct, but related developments: working-class ageing became seen as slightly less undesirable, and middle-class ageing as a great deal more undesirable.

The middle age of working people became associated to some limited extent with steadiness, reliability and respectability. When early twentieth-century employers were looking for women to work in domestic service, some specified that only the middle-aged should apply.[58] When they were looking for men to work with limited supervision, some made it clear that the middle aged would be preferred: a 'steady, middle-aged Man wanted to work up a milk round'; 'Middle-Aged Married Man Wanted' to work with horses on a farm.[59] In fact, the association between age, class and reliability persisted more powerfully than one might imagine. When mid twentieth-century employers were looking for women to work in domestic service and for men to work with limited supervision, they quite often stated a preference for the middle aged. 'Sand Quarry. – Man, over 40, used to all-yr.-round manual work in the open, to get & prepare sand for loading; must be used to working without direct supervision & be of regular attendance.'[60]

56. *Family Doctor*, 25 January 1890.
57. *Family Doctor*, 19 February 1910. See also *Daily Mail*, 5 January 1950.
58. *Barnsley Chronicle*, 25 March, 8 April 1911; *The Times*, 6 May 1915.
59. Wolverhampton, *Express and Star*, 5, 22 April 1911; *Birmingham Mail*, 11 June 1908.
60. *Express and Star*, 20 August 1947. Also *Mail on Sunday*, 6 October 1996.

The middle age of the middle class became associated much more than before with a combination of complacency and anxiety. It was a development whose origins can be traced once again to the very beginning of the century. 'Time was, and not so long ago,' claimed a correspondent to the *Lancet* in 1901, 'when a medical man was not much considered, not much trusted, and not often consulted by the people till he had arrived at a good age as to time and experience.' However, times had already begun to change, he maintained. 'Patients – i.e. patients in the higher platform of intelligence – very often come to look with suspicion at the medical man whose hair is white.'[61]

Manufacturers and advertisers were quick, as always, to seek to exploit these new anxieties. As will be seen in Chapter 4, the makers of hair dyes and restorers were particularly active. Readers of *Woman's Own* were warned in 1914 that. 'At a time when so many firms are dispensing with the services of their employees – the prematurely aged (by reason of their grey hair) are the first to go.'[62] Readers of the *Daily Sketch* were informed in 1959 that 'Healthy and abundant hair is a social and business asset'. However, care was needed to keep it that way. 'The young father in the picture has a splendid head of hair. But will it last well into middle age?'.[63]

These two developments – the slight satinisation of working-class ageing and the much more significant stigmatisation of middle-class ageing – helped to produce a growing convergence in popular ideas about what it was to be middle-aged. For during the course of the twentieth century, middle age was redefined so that those in their forties and fifties were seen as increasingly homogeneous. So whether they were male or female, middle-class or working-class, active or inactive, lucky or unlucky, they became associated in the public mind with the same curious combination of decay and anxiety, collapse and complacency.

The middle aged, it was believed, all tended to fall prey eventually to a broadly similar set of physical and psychological difficulties. The middle aged were all thought prone to corpulence, creaking joints, greying hair, failing eyesight, marital difficulties and depressive illness. Both men and women, it was maintained, tended to put on weight and turn grey. 'Beginning to look old as the result of thinning or greying locks has hindered many a man and woman's chances of advancement', it was claimed in 1930; 'it has even cost numbers their very livelihood, owing to their positions having been

61. 'SENEX' to *Lancet*, 31 August 1901.
62. *Woman's Own*, 11 April 1914. Also 18 July 1914.
63. *Daily Sketch*, 3 February 1959. Also *John Bull*, 6 May 1950.

given to younger-looking folk'.[64] Neither the active nor inactive
were immune. F. A. Hornibrook began the 1952 edition of his book,
The Culture of the Abdomen, with a dire warning.

> Between the trained athlete and the sedentary book-worm lies a great
> gulf across which age eventually throws a bridge where both meet in
> middle life, both burdened with enfeebled bodies, adipose deposits,
> pendulous bellies, constipated bowels and impaired mental activity.[65]

Women's magazines began to alert their readers to the perils of
'the dangerous forties': 'For most people, this is a time of readjust-
ment. A woman usually goes through the change of life and sees
her children leave home. A man realizes that he has been either a
success – or a failure.'[66]

In fact, it became increasingly common to associate middle age
explicitly with decline, decay and complacency. In 1935 a columnist
in the *Sunday Graphic* complained that,

> The impression prevails among millions still far away from the middle-
> line, that past forty there must be consciousness of departed virility,
> the power of enjoyment wilted and one must be aware of creeping
> senility with the dread of going ga-ga and being a confounded nuis-
> ance to folk around.[67]

Fifty years later, *Weekend* magazine published the results of a
National Opinion Poll survey into middle age. According to those
who were interviewed, the middle aged were regarded as relaxed
and in control, but with the tendency to lead 'a rather staid life style,
gardening or staying at home to watch TV or do some DIY'.[68]

The ways in which the term middle age and its derivatives were
used is most revealing. Middle age, it is clear, became associated
with stagnation, rancour and dullness.[69] Indeed, the terms 'middle-
aged' and 'middle-aged spread' became widely used, and widely
understood, synonyms for complacency and self-indulgence. 'Imper-
manence is the lot of all encyclopaedias', explained H. G. Wells in

64. *John Bull*, 18 January 1930. Also *Tit-Bits*, 27 February 1965.
65. F. A. Hornibrook, *The Culture of the Abdomen: The Cure of Obesity and Constipation*,
William Heinemann, London, 1952, p. 1.
66. *Woman*, 15 November 1958. Also Rev W. H. Elliott in *Sunday Graphic*, 22
February 1948.
67. Sir J. F. Fraser in *Sunday Graphic*, 7 July 1935.
68. *Weekend*, 15 October 1988. Also *Daily Mail*, 9 September 1985; *Sunday Times
Magazine*, 21 July 1996.
69. *Sunday Times Magazine*, 11 December 1994; Angus Wilson, *The Middle Age of
Mrs Eliot*, Penguin, 1961, p. 177; A. F. Robertson, 'A Middle-aged Romance', *Cornhill
Magazine*, 80, 1899, p. 377.

1931, and 'the Britannica shows now these marks of advanced maturity, of "middle-aged spread"'.[70] 'The head teacher may have been middle-aged,' remarked Walter Greenwood a few years later, 'but it was hard to tell because of her vigour.'[71] When the *Listener* magazine wished to compliment the television programme 'Tonight' in 1962, it argued that it displayed 'That impish sense of the ridiculous' which would always prevent it 'from acquiring the pompous middle-aged spread that so often accompanies success'.[72] When Janet Street-Porter launched her blistering attack on the 'grey' men running British television in the mid 1990s, she did so in terms of what she called the four Ms.

> A terminal blight has hit the British TV industry nipping fun in the bud, stunting our growth and severely restricting our development. This blight is management – the dreaded four Ms: male, middle-class, middle-aged and mediocre.[73]

The physical and psychological anxieties of middle age were reflected too in the jokes that were told about it. In his classic study of comic postcards, George Orwell described one of the 'conventions of the sex joke'.

> Sex-appeal vanishes at about the age of twenty-five. Well-preserved and good-looking people beyond their first youth are never represented. The amorous honeymooning couple reappear as the grim-visaged wife and hapless, mustachioed, red-nosed husband, no intermediate stage being allowed for.[74]

It is true that jokes about middle age tended to run to a formula. How do you know you're middle-aged? It's when you get out of the bath and are glad to see that the mirror is all steamed up. How do you know you're middle-aged? It's when you can't turn the TV set off or the au pair on. 'The funny thing about middle age is . . . you never reach it until you're past it.'[75] Sometimes the jokes became highly elaborate. 'A great deal of extremely useful work is being done by the Centre for Maturity Studies to tackle the problem of

70. *OED*, IX, p. 743.
71. W. Greenwood, *How the Other Man Lives*, Labour Book Service, London c. 1937, p. 202.
72. *OED*, IX, p. 743.
73. *Guardian*, 26 August 1995. Also *The Times*, 26 August 1995; *Independent*, 28 August 1995.
74. G. Orwell, *The Collected Essays, Journalism and Letters of George Orwell Volume II: My Country Right or Left 1940–1943*, S. Orwell and I. Angus (eds), Penguin, 1970, p. 186.
75. *The Victim's Guide to . . . Middle Age*, Exley Publications, n.p., 1993.

disaffected middle-aged people in our society today', reported a *Sunday Telegraph* columnist in 1994.

> It is all too easy for the rest of us to dismiss these people as 'obsolescents' or 'quaranteenagers' who are interested only in gin-and-tonic and adultery, but we ought to try to understand their real needs …
>
> Another charity called 'Middle Years Outreach' has set up a 24-hour Helpline for men and women to call in confidence and discuss their worries. 'We talk to the chaps and chapesses in their own language and we are never judgemental,' said the Rev Tony Trevor who runs the Helpline and also goes out into the streets to make contact with the middle-aged. 'In my experience, there are two things that concern them more than anything else,' he said. 'Cholesterol and parking spaces.'[76]

Individualisation

If physical failings, psychological anxieties and social stigmatisation were not enough, the middle aged soon had a further problem with which to contend. The difficulties of middle age came to be regarded not only as unpleasant and worrying but also as largely unnecessary. It became increasingly accepted during the course of the century that the middle aged, whether male or female, working-class or middle-class, could – and should – take responsibility for their own lives. It became increasingly accepted therefore that those who aged badly had largely – if not only – themselves to blame.

The message was hammered home time and time again. 'There is no need for the busy housewife to look old before her time if she takes reasonable, daily care of her appearance', insisted *Tit-Bits* in the mid 1930s.[77] 'I don't think that we can count our age by years at all', readers of the *Sunday Graphic* were assured in 1948.[78] Those who complain loudest about becoming middle-aged 'have usually done nothing to stay youthful', scolded television health expert Dr Miriam Stoppard in 1988.[79]

The message was clear: the middle aged got the middle age which they deserved.[80] To age well, all that was needed, it seemed,

---

76. *Sunday Telegraph*, 5 June 1994.   77. *Tit-Bits*, 23 February 1935.
78. *Sunday Graphic*, 14 March 1948.
79. *Weekend*, 15 October 1988. Also Consumers' Association, *Middle Age*, pp. 58–63; C. D'Souza, 'Age Cannot Wither Them', *Sunday Times, Style*, 27 August 1995; M. Heron, 'Old at 40, Young at 60', *Good Housekeeping*, May 1994.
80. *Sunday Times*, 21 August 1994.

was to use the appropriate medical and cosmetic aids, eat sparingly, exercise sensibly and think positively. It was a message that was aimed first at the comfortably-off, but was directed more and more – and apparently with more and more success – towards the less well-off and those ill-equipped in other respects to respond to its promptings.

The attack upon middle age was presented as a joint enterprise to be undertaken by manufacturers, advertisers, retailers and consumers, with the medical, pharmaceutical, beauty and fashion industries particularly keen to stress the growing opportunities for remedial action. From the 1930s onwards, the makers of products like Phyllosan, tonic wine and Dr Williams' Pink Pills promised to alleviate 'women's sufferings at middle life'[81] and to 'smooth out the problems of middle life'.[82] 'If, as you approach forty, you cannot have a body as supple as a young willow tree, you can at least keep it to its proper proportions, so that you are able to wear the modern flattering fashions with confidence.'[83] Indeed, a glance today through the pages of almost any newspaper or magazine will confirm the resilience, and apparent potency, of this type of appeal. As the publisher of *Your Prostate: What Every Man Over 40 Needs To Know Now!* explains, the book 'contains the latest up-to-date information on . . . how to protect yourself'.[84] How does fifty-five-year-old Gloria Hunniford manage to look so young, wonders the *Daily Mirror*.

Gloria pops the pills every morning and lists the names of what she calls her 'stalwarts'. 'The most important thing is Vitamin C, for hair, skin and nails,' she says. 'After that, a pure Vitamin E is truly marvellous for hair and skin and it's a really good internal healer.

So too is Oil of Evening Primrose. Then I take a thing called Urticalcin. It's very good for osteoporosis.

Next I have a thing called Tri-Plus or CH3. Barbara Cartland calls it the brain pill but it's good for all-round energy.

The latest one I've tried is called Ginkgo. It stimulates the blood to the brain and is good for short-term and long-term memory.[85]

The claims of cosmetics and corsetry manufacturers proved remarkably similar to those of the pharmaceutical industry. The promises made by the cosmetics industry are well known, and easily

81. *John Bull*, 26 April 1930.
82. *Tit-Bits*, 26 January 1935. Also 15 March 1930; *Sunday Graphic*, 15 February 1931; *Woman*, 2 April 1938.
83. *John Bull*, 23 March, 6 April 1940; *Sun*, 11 October 1966; J. Benson, *The Rise of Consumer Society in Britain, 1880–1980*, Longman, 1994, p. 48.
84. *Sunday Times*, 23 January 1994; *Observer*, 27 February 1994.
85. *Daily Mirror*, December 1995.

derided. 'If, at forty, you possess a "middle-aged" complexion, it is entirely your own fault', insisted the makers of Mercolized Wax in 1931.[86] 'She's 40 but looks 29', claimed the makers of 'Facial Youth' cream a few years later.[87] 'Maybe it begins at 30. Maybe 40', warned Estée Lauder in 1994. 'One day you realise your skin is just not as resilient. Now we can help you bring it back.'[88] The promises made by the corsetry industry are less well known, but little more convincing. From the earliest years of the century, both men and women were urged to counter 'the increasing ill-health and tiredness caused by a sedentary life and advancing years'.[89] Happily, help was at hand.

> For women whose figures have grown matronly and full, it is quite worth while having well-cut under-bodices. . . . They should be made so as to hold the figure trim and neat. It is not nice to see the form floppy and spread out under a thin blouse.[90]

Fashion was also important. For whether she bought ready-made clothes, had them made, or made her own, it was important that the middle-aged women dressed appropriately. There were three basic rules that she should follow, suggested the *Bristol Observer* in 1911: 'To dress in accordance with her income; to dress in accordance with her age and position; and to dress appropriately to the occasion.'[91] Naturally, notions of what constituted appropriate dress changed over the years. At the beginning of the century, middle-aged women were urged to cover up and wear dark colours. Readers of *The Lady* were told in 1911 that,

> Barker's have for years specialised in Black wear, and because this colour is undoubtedly the most suitable and becoming for the Matron approaching middle age, or of middle age, it has followed that more Matrons visit Barker's Show-rooms than is usually the case.[92]

In the 1960s, the middle aged were advised to eschew 'safe' colours such as fawn, beige and mid-grey: middle-aged women with grey or silver hair would be better advised, it was felt, to wear clothes that were blue, pink, lilac or hyacinth.[93]

86. *Sunday Graphic*, 8 March 1931.   87. *Woman*, 19 March 1938.
88. *Marie Claire*, April 1994.
89. *Picture Post*, 9 December 1939. Also *John Bull*, 6 April 1940; *Woman's Own*, 3 January 1914; *Woman's Way*, 23, 30 March 1935; *Woman*, 12 February 1938, 20 April 1940, *John Bull*, 28 January, 30 September 1950.
90. *Woman's Own*, 3 January 1914.   91. *Bristol Observer*, 8 April 1911.
92. *The Lady*, 2 February 1911, Also *Woman's Own*, 7 February, 26 September, 7 November 1914, 3 July, 16 October 1915.
93. *Woman*, 16 April 1960. Also *Medical News*, 4 January 1963.

However, it was not just those with commercial interests in targeting the middle-aged market that stressed the opportunities for remedial action. So too did a growing number of doctors, journalists, politicians, enthusiasts and other commentators. There had always been one or two medical mavericks urging the importance of moderation and self-discipline. The middle aged should eat sparingly, it was suggested in 1876: 'Everybody who has passed the age of fifty (or thereabouts) with a fairly unimpaired constitution will act wisely in diminishing his daily allowance of solid food.'[94] Such views became much more widely disseminated during the course of the twentieth century. In a guide to *Middle Age and Old Age* published in 1925, readers were warned how careful they should be.

> The theory that food 'builds up' or 'keeps up' the strength, which monopolises the field of the present, and leads to all manner of fantastic excess both in health and disease, leaves altogether out of the picture the exhausting labour to which the digestive and assimilating organs are condemned by the practice which the theory implies. ... There are more people floated into their coffins on a flood of beef-tea and milk than ever arrive there by the ravages of disease.[95]

By the second half of the century the middle aged, along with everybody else, knew that they should restrict their calorific intake. Readers of *Every Woman's Book of Love* were advised that, 'The man or woman who has reached middle age no longer needs a "full diet"; actually he or she will do far better on one that is light but sustaining and will not overtax the digestive organs.'[96] Readers of the *Sunday Times* were told in 1995 that although 'a woman of 50 is still a young woman, ... the menopause does bring some problems. Fortunately, a well-adapted diet will help. Eating lots of cheese, for example, will help prevent osteoporosis (brittle bones), which is caused by calcium loss. So will cutting down on alcohol and coffee.'[97]

Sensible diet needed to be complemented by sensible exercise. There had always been some who urged the importance of exercise and good posture. They helped to delay ageing, it was claimed, and had 'a very decided effect upon the mind'.[98] Once again, such views

---

94. T. King Chambers, *A Manual of Diet in Health and Disease*, Smith, Elder & Co, London, 1876, p. 227. Also *Family Doctor*, 19 March 1910.

95. L. Williams, *Middle Age and Old Age*, Oxford University Press, Oxford, 1925, pp. 8–9. Also *Sunday Graphic*, 25 October 1931. Cf. *Woman's Weekly*, 20 March 1920.

96. *Every Woman's Book*, p. 164. Also *Daily Sketch*, 6 January 1970.

97. *Sunday Times, Style*, 21 May 1995.

98. *Woman's Own*, 9 May 1914. Also *Family Doctor*, 19 April 1890.

became much more widely disseminated during the course of the twentieth century. Exercise was vital, insisted *Woman's Own* in 1914:

> from unmarried and married alike, an alert and ready responsiveness is looked for unless they wish to be considered as 'getting on', and one of the signs of youthfullness [sic] and freshness of mind is seen in the upright and gracefully firm carriage of the body.[99]

Exercise was vital, insisted more and more commentators during the second half of the century. In *The Culture of the Abdomen*, F. A. Hornibrook urged the need for proper exercise, and warned his readers that 'YOUR WAIST LINE IS YOUR LIFE LINE'.[100] Other enthusiasts waxed almost lyrical.

> It is . . . only by accustoming himself, by easy degrees, to unwonted exercise that the citizen beyond middle age can derive the indubitable benefit to be found in exercise among the mountains. Not only, with due precaution, will his flabby muscles be made firm and strong, but his breathing power will be improved. . . . Dr Hermann Weber, of London, states that mountain exercise has a beneficial influence on the hair, and that the greyness of many persons in hair and beard has been diminished by a mountain tour.[101]

In 1950, an editorial in the *Daily Graphic* reflected on the story of eighty-four-year-old Charlie Hart who had braved bad weather to go on a sixteen-mile run. 'Activity,' it concluded, 'whether of mind or body, keeps old age at bay. Don't overtax your strength – but keep on doing the things you know you can do.'[102] For as a 1965 advertisement for the book *Be Fit at 40: The Mature Man's Guide to Physical Fitness* pointed out, 'The average man pays more attention to his car – which he can get serviced and replaced – than to his body which he cannot'.[103] Indeed, by the 1990s, it was not just the body that needed a workout. So too did the face.

> Eva Fraser, doyenne of facial exercises, is opening a Facial Workout Studio next week in Kensington . . .
> So how do you work out your face? And why should you bother, anyway? 'The method doesn't stop ageing, but it certainly delays it. It lifts one's spirits and makes one more confident,' claims Ms Fraser.[104]

99. *Woman's Own*, 9 May 1914.   100. Hornibrook, *Culture*, pp. 13, 19.
101. Hepworth and Featherstone, *Surviving Middle Age*, p. 61. Also *John Bull*, 25 February 1950; *Every Woman's Book*, p. 164.
102. *Daily Graphic*, 18 September 1950. Also *Woman*, 11 February 1950.
103. *Tit-Bits*, 15 May 1965. Also *Daily Mail*, 3 May 1965; *Guardian*, 3 March 1995; *Woman's Own*, 29 July 1996.
104. *Independent on Sunday*, 15 October 1995.

Yet even sensible diet and regular exercise might not be sufficient to stave off the ravages of middle age. There was one further
thing that was needed: positive thinking. Indeed, the belief that the
ageing process could be slowed, and even arrested and reversed, by
individual effort and strength of will has a remarkably long pedi-
gree. As the *Family Doctor* insisted time and again around the turn
of the century, 'Growing old is largely a matter of habit or belief,
and lack of knowledge of how to prevent it'.[105]

In fact, those offering advice on how to cope with middle age
became increasingly enthusiastic about the benefits to be derived
from positive thinking and the adoption of an appropriate lifestyle.
Women were told from the earliest years of the century that they
'may become more attractive as the years go on, even the plainest
acquiring beauty as the result of pure life and aspiring character'.[106]

> Attend any gathering at which are present many women on the fur-
> ther side of middle age, and you will see numbers of them showing
> considerable attractions of face and personality – charms that have
> become ripened by time, and characters rounded out and beautified
> by growth and experience.[107]

For as George Orwell put it in his celebrated aphorism, 'At 50,
everyone has the face he deserves'.[108]

At first, such proselytisation was confined largely to specialist
magazines and self-help guides intended for an upper and middle-
class readership. The ageing process defied generalisation, those
thinking of marrying were assured in 1910: 'There are old matrons
of twenty, and coquettes of forty, and old men of twenty, and old
fops of sixty.'[109] The ageing process could be slowed substantially,
readers of *Old Age Deferred* were assured in 1922. The book concluded with 'Twelve Commandments for the Preservation of Youth,
and the Attainment of a Green Old Age', one of which read as
follows: 'avoid mental emotions, and also worries about things that
have happened and cannot be altered, as well as about things that
may happen. Never . . . say unpleasant things, and . . . avoid listen-
ing to such, if possible.'[110]

105. Reference mislaid. Also *Family Doctor*, 7 May, 4 June 1910.
106. *Family Doctor*, 4 June 1910.
107. *Family Doctor*, 7 May 1910. Also *Lancet*, 2 December 1905.
108. *Guardian*, 1 August 1994.
109. *Family Doctor*, 3 September 1910. Also *Lancet*, 2 December 1905; *Woman's Own*, 9 May 1914.
110. A. Lorand, *Old Age Deferred: The Causes of Old Age and Its Postponement by Hygienic and Therapeutic Measures*, Davis, Philadelphia 1922, pp. 457–8. Also *Woman's Own*, 9, 23 May 1914; S. Trent, *Women Over Forty*, Duckworth, 1935; Featherstone and Hepworth, *Surviving Middle Age*, pp. 72–9.

These and similar arguments were put with increasing insistence and conviction during the second half of the century. Readers of books such as *The Wonderful Crisis of Middle Age* were told in 1973 about the life-enhancing opportunities of the middle years, the chance, it was claimed, 'to do your own thing' and 'to become most truly alive and yourself'.[111] Women 'of "a certain age" facing, undergoing or emerging from the midlife rite of passage – menopause' were urged in the early 1990s to enrol in a five-day workshop on 'The Wild Woman Archetype' where they could learn, 'to facilitate and celebrate the wild, irrational and untame-able archetypes of the truly feminine'.[112]

However as time went by, the importance of positive thinking was publicised a good deal more broadly. Women's magazines and national newspapers began to preach the virtues of the correct mental outlook.[113] In 1938, Evelyn Home replied sharply to a thirty-eight-year-old woman who feared that life was slipping by her.

> Age does not only mean the loss of physical elasticity. It means greater understanding, greater tolerance and, above all, the possibility of creating something worth while now that you know which things are worthless.[114]

Twenty years later, *Woman* magazine advised its readers to cope with 'the dangerous forties' by thinking and acting positively: 'Half the battle is to be aware of the dangers of the forties and to take action to avoid them.'[115] It was not difficult to lose weight if one had the right attitude of mind: 'Some people accept a spread, middle-aged or otherwise, philosphically; others try to get rid of it.'[116] As a columnist in the *Sunday Graphic* had reassured his readers in the mid 1930s, 'There are more opportunities to be happy after forty than before forty. ... At forty you ought to be sane, sound and seasoned.'[117]

Gradually, however, the idea that the middle aged could be sane, sound and seasoned gave way to the thought that they might be slim, sensuous and sexy. Newspapers, both serious and popular, began to report endlessly on public figures who seemed able to defy the years. The *Sunday Graphic* revealed in 1950 that film star

111. Featherstone and Hepworth, *Surviving Middle Age*, pp. 156–7.
112. Physis Archetypal and Applied Psychology Programme, *The Wild Woman Archetype*, 1994.
113. For a much earlier example, see *Daily Mail*, 9 September 1905.
114. *Woman*, 26 March 1938. 115. *Woman*, 15 November 1958.
116. *Woman*, 29 November 1958.
117. *Sunday Graphic*, 7 July 1935. Also 9 August 1931, 11 January 1948, 5 February 1950.

Joan Blondell was happy to be forty,[118] *Tit-Bits* described Doris Day
in 1965 as 'The blonde who is finding that life really begins at
40',[119] and the *Daily Mail* announced ten years later that ex-Queen
Soraya of Persia was 'Showing few signs of her 42 years'. (It was just
as well: 'her escort Francesco Napolino is 20 years her junior and
a university student'.[120]) The *Sunday Mirror*'s 1995 feature on the
actress Kate O'Mara is typical of the genre.

> Trying on a pair of black fishnet stockings and teetering on lethal
> stiletto heels, Kate O'Mara is clearly enjoying herself. 'How do I
> look, then?' she purrs, arching the famous eyebrows, narrowing those
> lynx-like green eyes and giving her wickedest half-smile. There can
> be only one answer – *Absolutely Fabulous*, darling. . . . And, at 55, she
> still has the 24-inch waist, flawless, unlined complexion and the sort
> of figure most women half her age – not to mention the champagne-
> swilling Patsy – would kill for.[121]

Sportsmen too showed what might be achieved. Indeed, the early-
mid 1990s saw a plethora of stories with headlines such as 'Golden
boys still fighting fit'[122] and 'Old hands who came to grips with
middle-aged spread'.[123] 'Sport used to be something you messed
about with before you grew up and got a proper job', explained the
Independent.

> Now there are wrinklies everywhere. Desmond Douglas, 11 times
> English table tennis champion, and well into his thirty-ninth year, is
> set on making an international comeback. Horse racing has Piggott
> and Carson still riding towards the sunset at the ages of 58 and 51.
> Nigel Mansell delivered an IndyCar world championship to go with
> his Formula One crown at the age of 40.[124]

However, it was George Foreman's winning of the world heavy-
weight boxing championship in 1994 that drove journalists to new
heights of hyperbole. 'Foreman fortifies the over forties', declared
the *Guardian*.

> It used to be Phyllosan that fortified the over-40s; George Foreman
> relied on triple burgers, apple pie and ice cream, and at 45 years and

118. *Sunday Graphic*, 5 February 1950.   119. *Tit-Bits*, 16 January 1965.
120. *Daily Mail*, 7 January 1975.
121. *Sunday Mirror*, 26 March 1995. Also *Daily Mail*, 5 September 1960; *Weekend*,
5 November 1988; *Guardian*, 1 September 1995; *Daily Express*, 26 July 1996; *Independent*, 29 July 1996.
122. *Guardian*, 7 November 1994.
123. *Observer*, 2 January 1994. Also *Guardian*, 1 September 1994; *The Times*, 13 May
1995; *Daily Telegraph*, 21 July 1995; *Independent*, 27 July 1995.
124. *Independent*, 23 January 1994.

10 months has become the oldest world boxing champion in history. . . . 'Anything you desire you can make happen. Just like the song When You Wish Upon A Star, your dreams come true,' said an exuberant Foreman after knocking out his 26-year-old opponent Michael Moorer in the tenth round of Saturday night's fight in Las Vegas.[125]

There was one further development. Whereas celebrities and sportsmen and women were depicted first simply as objects of envy, they were presented more and more as objects both of envy and of possible emulation.[126] 'It's easy to keep young', urged *Tit-Bits* in 1935.[127] Women who are healthy and cheerful have the fewest wrinkles, maintained the *Sunday Graphic* in 1948. 'This is proof that the greatest help is the youthful spirit.'[128]

Such arguments were taken up, repeated and refined. 'Age isn't a matter of years', claimed the makers of Phillips Tonic Yeast in 1962: 'It's a question of how old you *feel* and that is largely up to you.'[129] The menopause is worse if you worry about it, suggested the *Daily Sketch* in 1970.[130] Forty is a turning point one way or another, explained *Weekend* magazine in 1988: 'Some say it's when life begins, others that it's the start of middle age.'[131]

> For the middle-aged, life has never been so rewarding. They keep fit with jogging, aerobics and other sports, and lead the rush for the latest fashions in clothes and cooking. They will even go round the world on an adventure trip at the drop of a premium bond.[132]

Malcolm Bradbury saw clearly what was happening. Writing in the mid 1990s, he pointed out that,

> 40 has become the cusp because it is, roughly speaking, the essential midlife moment when feeling good and young gives way to feeling bad and old. And unusually, our present culture is one where we're supposed – in fact politically encouraged – to feel good. We ought to be fit: get out the running shoes, put on the tracksuit, grab the surf-board, chase off to the tennis game, the marathon, the gym or the pitch.[133]

No doubt, such positive thinking brought its own rewards. Yet it could also foster feelings of impotence and resentment. For as

---

125. *Guardian*, 7 November 1994.   126. *Sun*, 7 March 1985.
127. *Tit-Bits*, 26 January 1935.   128. *Sunday Graphic*, 15 February 1948.
129. *Today*, 27 January 1962.   130. *Daily Sketch*, 20 January 1970.
131. *Weekend*, 5 November 1988.   132. *Weekend*, 3 December 1988.
133. M. Bradbury, 'Stuck in the Middle', *Sunday Times*, 9 April 1995. Also *Guardian*, 17 February 1994; *Independent*, 29 July 1996; G. Sheehy, 'Yes, Life Really *Does* Begin at 40', *Daily Mail*, 4 May 1996.

Sunday Times columnist Lynn Barber complained at almost exactly the same time,

> There does seem to be an enormous conspiracy at the moment . . .
> to pretend that middle-aged women are just as pretty as young ones.
> . . . Hardly a week goes by in which some well-wisher doesn't give me
> a little lecture about the advantages of HRT and the terrible dangers
> of 'letting myself go'. Why *can't* I let myself go? I feel I've earned the
> right to, I've done my stint on the treadmill of attraction . . .
> What is so unfair was that when I was young, nobody hinted for a
> moment that women over 40 were meant to be attractive. So I went
> through my twenties and thirties assuming there would eventually be
> a cut-off point where I could stop wearing high-heels and struggling
> to fit into a size 12. I didn't exactly welcome it but I didn't resent it
> either: it was just how life was. Then beastly Jane Fonda and tiresome
> Joan Collins and hateful Raquel Welch changed all the rules and
> now there is no limit to how long you are supposed to go on flashing
> your cleavage and baring your thighs.[134]

It is clear then that the twentieth century has seen a transformation in the meanings that are attached to middle age. It has been defined increasingly in chronological terms, associated indelibly with physical and psychological decline, yet regarded as more and more avoidable given the adoption of the appropriate remedial action. Middle age has been at once demonised, homogenised and individualised.

A working definition of middle age

This transformation makes it difficult to provide even a working definition of middle age, and difficult therefore to calculate the number, and proportion, of the population that should be described as middle-aged at different times over the past hundred years.

There are a number of complications. It has to be decided first whether to define middle age in its own terms, as a period with distinct and distinctive features, or to define it residually, as the period which is left sandwiched between adulthood and old age or, as some suggest, between youth and old age.[135] It has to be decided too how far it is possible to adopt a definition that can be applied with equal validity to men and women, the upper class, middle class and working class, and those from the beginning and end of the century – as well as those from ethnic communities and those living in different parts of the country. It has to be decided finally whether

134. *Sunday Times, Style and Travel*, 29 May 1994.   135. *OED*, IX, p. 743.

it is best to adopt a biological, psychological/social or chronological approach, and whether it is possible to collect the necessary
indicators of biological, psychological/social or chronological ageing
for the hundred years or so that form the subject of this book.

Nonetheless, it is believed that progress can be made. It will be
argued that while a biological approach promises the most objective, and a psychological/social approach the most sensitive definition of middle age, neither can be used effectively in a longitudinal
study such as this. It will be suggested therefore that the difficulties
of distinguishing between the objective and subjective, the know-
able and unknowable, mean that it is the chronological definition
that must be used. Thus in this book, middle age will be defined
simply, but it is believed constructively, as the years between the
ages of forty and sixty, and it will be measured by using the mass
of census material that has been collected since the beginning of
the century.

It can certainly be shown that the biological definition of middle
age offers few attractions to the social historian of ageing. For
however thorough the collection of physiological, anthropometric,
morbidity, mortality and similar data, and however sophisticated
their subsequent analysis and interpretation, they can tell us little
about the way in which middle age should be defined. The decline
of muscular strength, the loss of flexibility and the increasing likelihood of cardio-vascular disorders exemplify, but do not define, what
it is to be middle-aged.[136]

The psychological/social definition appears a good deal more
promising. The difficulty is to avoid lapsing into the common – and
common-sense – view that middle age, like old age, is simply a matter of self-definition. 'You're as old as you feel', we are told: 'age
is all in the mind'.[137] Such self-definition seems a most attractive pro-
position – especially as one begins to grow older. However, it cannot
be sustained in any serious way. We are not as old as we feel, as old
as we claim to feel – or as old as other people believe us to be.[138]
Indeed, it is striking that when those in their middle years seek to
define themselves as something other than middle-aged, they do
so by denying that they are middle-aged. They deny their middle

136. Briggs, 'Biological Ageing'; Consumers' Association, *Middle Age*, esp. pp. 57–
69; J. E. Fixx, *The Complete Book of Running*, Penguin, 1977, p. 106; B. Tulloch, *The
Complete Distance Runner*, Panther, 1983, p. 216.

137. M. Fiske, *Middle Age: The Prime of Life?*, Harper & Row, London, pp. 22–3.

138. Greer, *The Change*, pp. 6–7. Also p. 272; A. S. Rossi, 'Life-span Theories and
Women's Lives', *Signs: Journal of Women in Culture and Society*, 6, 1980, pp. 12–13.

age, in other words, by reference to their own, and other people's, middle age.[139]

Even if the self-definitional approach to middle age could be defended conceptually, it cannot be applied empirically. There seems no way of identifying, measuring and quantifying the ways in which those in their middle years have, or have not, defined themselves as middle-aged during the course of the twentieth century. The self-definitional approach to middle age suffers, it must be concluded, from the very subjectivity that constitutes its chief attraction.

If the psychological/social approach to middle age is to prove historically tenable, it needs to move from self-definition to a procedure that is less subjective, can be applied more or less consistently at different periods of time, and is amenable to some degree of quantification. It would be possible, one might think, to define middle age economically (in terms of work, earnings and retirement) or to define it demographically (in terms of life expectancy, family structure and family relationships).[140]

It is certainly tempting to try to define middle age in economic terms, to argue, for example, that middle age begins when earnings peak and ends, perhaps, when they begin to decline. However, such an approach throws into sharp relief the difficulties of finding a definition of middle age that comes close to encompassing the very different experiences of men and women, and of those in white-collar and manual occupations. It is well known that men's and women's work patterns were rarely the same, and well known too that whereas white-collar workers usually received a series of age and/or service-related increments which meant that their earnings peaked when they were in their late thirties or early forties, manual workers tended to attain their highest earnings when they were in their late teens or early twenties.[141]

It is also tempting to try to define middle age demographically, to claim, for example, that middle age occurs between certain fixed points in the life cycle. Such an approach would mean, not unreasonably, that as life expectancy increased, so middle age occurred later and later. However, such an approach brings its own, apparently intractable, difficulties. For one thing, it would raise again the problem of universalising the experiences of the two sexes and the different classes. For another, it would raise the problem of identifying the fixed points in the life cycle that can be applied with equal validity

---

139. *Cf. Daily Mail*, 4 May 1935, WOH, Mrs O.   140. Greer, *The Change*, p. 49.
141. Rossi, 'Life-span Theories', pp. 12–13.

in periods of high and low life expectancy, periods of high and low earnings and so on. Indeed, it seems that whichever fixed points are selected, there is no way of defining middle age satisfactorily in terms of life expectancy, family structure and family relationships.

If the psychological/social approach to defining middle age is to prove historically tenable, it will do so, it seems, on the basis of a chronological approach. This is not to suggest, of course, that defining middle age chronologically removes all potential difficulties. It most assuredly does not. It leaves unresolved, for instance, the problem of finding a definition that can be applied satisfactorily to both sexes, to all classes, and to those living in the early twentieth century, the late twentieth century and all points in-between. Yet whatever its conceptual limitations and ahistorical rigidities, a chronologically based definition of middle age does possess two distinct advantages. It corresponds closely to contemporary usage, and it can be applied empirically to the social history of twentieth-century ageing.[142]

It is proposed therefore that the working definition of middle age to be used in this book will be chronologically based. It seems indisputable that of the various ages at which middle age might be said to start, the most useful is certainly forty; it has been seen after all that the onset of middle age was placed increasingly commonly, in fact almost unthinkingly, at the age of forty. However, it is a good deal more difficult to know which of the various ages at which middle age might be said to end will prove to be the most tenable. For although it became increasingly accepted that old age began with retirement from paid employment, there was no corresponding agreement that this was also the point at which middle age ended. What then is the student of middle age to do? It does seem that on balance the most appropriate point at which to end middle age is sixty, the age at which demographers, social scientists and market researchers often tended to divide the middle aged from the elderly. It follows therefore that in this book middle age is defined as the twenty-year period between the ages of forty and sixty – or to be more precise between the ages of forty and fifty-nine.

However, the adoption of this definition raises a further complication. Twenty years is a long period of anybody's life, and as Alice Rossi argues, 'the very broad definitions of middle age as a twenty-to-twenty-five-year phase of the life span must be abandoned, and research must work instead with narrow age ranges within which

142. Rossi, 'Life-span Theories', pp. 16, 20.

known biological changes are taking place which might illuminate
or be illuminated by psychological and social factors'.[143] It has been
decided therefore that it will be helpful to divide the twenty-year
period of middle age into two: early middle age, the years between
forty and forty-nine; and late middle age, the years between fifty
and fifty-nine. Such a division is arbitrary perhaps but it is convenient, has an appealing symmetry and is consistent with the common
view that fifty, like forty and sixty, marked a significant stage in the
course of the life cycle.[144] By the 1990s,

> Anyone choosing a birthday card is confronted with a dizzying array
> of gags that would have had George Orwell blushing to his boots . . .
> each decade – 30, 40, 50, 60 – is greeted with a barrage of jokes
> about sex, about how there's less of it, it's not so much fun, about
> bits dropping off.[145]

The number of the middle aged

Armed with this working definition of middle age, it is possible to
provide estimates of the number, and proportion, of the population
that should be described as middle-aged at ten-yearly intervals since
the beginning of the twentieth century. For whatever reservations
the compilers of the nineteenth-century census had about the accur-
acy of the information they were able to provide about age,[146] there
is no doubt that the reliability of the census improved immeasurably during the course of the twentieth century.[147] Indeed, it is commonly accepted that the census provides an unparalleled source
of information that can be used to explore a surprisingly wide
range of aspects of modern British economic, social and cultural
history.[148]

Figures 2.1 and 2.2 draw upon this information to show the
number and gender of the middle-aged population. The simplicity
of these figures must not be allowed to conceal the significance of
the developments which they reveal. They demonstrate, really for

143. Rossi, 'Life-span Theories', p. 18.
144. H. Ogilvie, *Fifty: An Approach to the Problems of Middle Age*, Max Parish, London,
1962; A Country Doctor, *Facing Retirement: A Guide for the Middle Aged and Elderly*,
Allen and Unwin, London, 1964; R. Harris and L. J. Frankel (eds), *Guide to Fitness
after Fifty*, Plenum Press, London, 1977; *Sunday Times*, 24 August 1994.
145. *Sunday Times*, 21 August 1994.
146. *Census of England and Wales*, 1891, *General Report*, pp. 27–8.
147. *Census of England and Wales*, 1901, *General Report*, pp. 51–64; 1921, *General
Report*, p. 80.
148. J. Benson, *The Working Class in Britain, 1850–1939*, Longman, 1989, pp. 3–4.

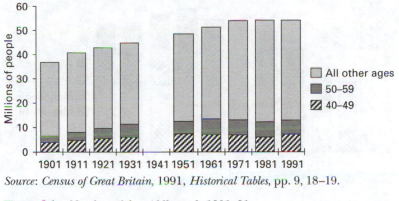

Source: *Census of Great Britain*, 1991, *Historical Tables*, pp. 9, 18–19.

Figure 2.1   *Numbers of the middle aged, 1901–91*

the first time, that the last hundred years have witnessed a major, albeit largely unremarked, transformation in the size and significance of the middle-aged population.[149]

Figure 2.1 shows, not very surprisingly, that as the population grew, so too did the number of the middle aged. The number of people aged between 40 and 59 all but doubled during the first ninety years of the century: from under 7 million in 1901, to over 13 million in 1991. The growth was greatest among the late middle aged: whereas the number of people in their forties grew by 87 per cent (from 3.9 million to 7.3 million), the number of those in their fifties increased by 115 per cent (from 2.7 million to 5.8 million). In fact, the middle-aged population of the late twentieth century was larger than the entire population of the country had been in the early years of the nineteenth century.

Nor is this all. For Figure 2.1 shows too that there was an increase in the proportion, as well as the number, of the population that were middle-aged. The proportion of the population aged between 40 and 59 increased by a third: from 18 per cent in 1901, to 24 per cent in 1991. The growth was greatest between 1911 and 1921 (due no doubt to the slaughter of young men in the Great War), and greatest generally among the late middle aged; whereas the proportion of the population in their forties grew by just over a quarter (from 11 per cent to 14 per cent) between 1911 and 1941, the proportion in their fifties increased by almost 60 per cent (from 7 per cent to 11 per cent). These were crucial developments:

149. Cf. the remarks in *Report Economic and Financial Problems*, 1954, p. 96.

34   *Prime Time*

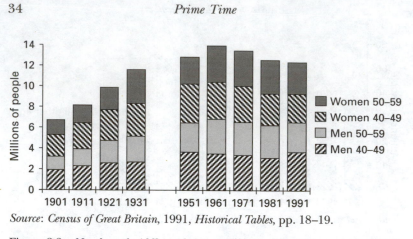

Source: *Census of Great Britain*, 1991, *Historical Tables*, pp. 18–19.

Figure 2.2   *Numbers of middle-aged men and women, 1901–91*

they meant that in 1911 the middle aged made up a fifth, and from 1931 a quarter or so of the entire British population.

Figure 2.2 shows, perhaps not surprisingly, that there were nearly always more women than men among the middle-aged population. The imbalance was particularly pronounced during the first thirty years of the century, when women outnumbered men by between 5 and 19 per cent; there was always a considerable excess of women in their forties, and usually an excess of women in their fifties. The imbalance became less pronounced during the second half of the century. Between 1961 and 1991, women outnumbered men by between only 2 and 6 per cent: there was usually a small excess of women in their forties, and usually a significant excess of women in their fifties. These developments too were of major importance: they provided the demographic context within which middle-aged men and women lived, worked, formed their relationships and thought about the future.

It is a great deal more difficult to disaggregate the middle aged according to social class. It would be easy of course if the classes could be defined and measured by occupation, and if the middle aged were distributed equally between occupations. If this were the case, all that would need to be done would be to adjust the available occupationally-based estimates of class size in the light of the figures for the middle-aged population that are provided in Figure 2.1.

The trouble is that it is by no means universally accepted that the classes can be defined and measured by occupation, and that it would be most surprising to find that the middle aged were distributed equally between the classes. It will be shown in the chapter which follows that life expectancy varied according to social class, and this meant that particularly in the early years of the century those from the working class were less likely than those from the middle and upper classes to survive into their forties and fifties.

However, it is one thing to show that the middle aged were not distributed equally between the classes, it is another to know how to allow for, and quantify, this unequal distribution. It would be possible, one might think, to use geographical distribution as a guide to class distribution. After all, the compilers of the census were perfectly well aware that the age structure of the population was different in different parts of the country. They reported in 1921, for example, that early middle-aged men were to be found disproportionately in urban areas and the north of England, late middle-aged men in rural areas and the south of England, and middle-aged women of all ages in London, the home counties and the south of England.[150]

Yet there seems no way of using such information to calculate age/class distribution, no way of identifying certain ages and classes with certain parts of the country. All that can be done therefore is to take the available occupationally-based statistics of class size, and adjust them in the light of the figures for the middle-aged population that were used in constructing Figure 2.1. When this is done, it reveals that while the working class always contained more of the middle aged – and more of all ages – than the other two classes, the gap narrowed during the course of the century. It suggests that whereas at the beginning of the century the working class contained 75 per cent (and probably fewer) of those in their forties and fifties, by the end of the century it contained 60 per cent (and probably many fewer) of those who are defined in this book as middle-aged.

This is not to deny, of course, that middle age remains peculiarly resistant to clear definition and reliable quantification. Indeed, such conceptual and empirical complications will continue to beset those interested in the history of middle age. It has been decided, however, that a chronological definition appears to provide the best – indeed the only practical – approach to the quantification of middle age. So armed with a definition of middle age as the years between the ages of forty and fifty-nine, it has been possible to estimate the

150. *Census of England and Wales, 1921, General Report*, pp. 65–71. Also 1911, vol. xviii, p. xii; 1951, *General Report*, p. 95.

number, and proportion, of the population who were middle-aged in the years that the census was taken. Such a procedure reveals the growing, albeit almost completely overlooked, importance of the middle aged in twentieth-century Britain. It is time that their history was written.

CHAPTER THREE

Health

The health of the middle aged has received a good deal of attention, some of it scholarly, some of it popular, some of it contradictory – and much of it highly misleading.[1] As was seen in the previous
chapter, it became increasingly accepted that the middle aged
tended to suffer a universal and substantial, albeit more or less
avoidable, decline in their physical capacity and psychological well-
being. Middle age, explained the Consumers' Association in 1976,
was 'a dangerous time for men from the point of view of health and
a difficult time for women'.[2] Such dangers and difficulties led very
often, it was believed, to feelings of failure and inadequacy as the
middle aged struggled to adapt to the undeniable, undesirable and
increasingly visible signs of their physical, intellectual and psychological deterioration.[3]

It is the purpose of this chapter to examine, and challenge, the
validity of these, and similar beliefs about middle-aged deterioration. For it is a good deal more difficult to generalise about the
relationship between age and health – and between age, health and
individual responsibility – than many existing studies would lead
one to suppose. So although it will be conceded that middle age
saw some decline in physical capacity, intellectual ability and psychological well-being, it will be argued – and argued most strongly
– that such deterioration was neither as universal nor as substantial

---

1. Health, of course, is difficult either to define or to measure. See H. Jones,
Health and Society in Twentieth-century Britain, Longman, 1994, pp. 1–3.

2. Consumers' Association, *Living Through Middle Age*, Consumers' Association, 1976,
p. 57. Also J. L. Horn and G. Donaldson, 'On the Myth of Intellectual Decline in
Adulthood', *American Psychologist*, October 1976, p. 707.

3. M. Hepworth and M. Featherstone, *Surviving Middle Age*, Blackwell, Oxford, 1982,
pp. 5–11. Cf. T. R. Cole, *The Journey of Life: A Cultural History of Aging in America*,
Cambridge University Press, Cambridge, 1992, p. 95.

as is usually suggested. It will be shown rather that the health of the middle aged improved during the course of the century, and that with gender differences growing wider between the ages of forty and sixty, these were years that saw a divergence, rather than a convergence, in levels of physical, intellectual and psychological well-being. It will be suggested, in other words, that the middle aged were less likely to get the middle age which they deserved than the middle age which they probably expected.

Decline

It is not as easy as it seems to show that health declined between adulthood and middle age. There are two major complications. It is often difficult to distinguish between health, fitness and well-being,[4] and it is sometimes almost impossible to differentiate between age and generation. So unless every effort is made to compare the health of the same generation at different times, rather than of different generations at the same time, what appears to be a change in health between adulthood and middle age may be no more than a change between the adults of one generation and the middle aged of the preceding generation.

There is no denying of course that middle age saw some decline in physical capacity. Although it is sometimes extremely difficult to distinguish satisfactorily between the physiological, psychological, environmental, economic, social and other determinants of physical well-being, there is no doubt that age brought with it some physical and sensory decline and a certain increased vulnerability to disease.

It has always been known that physical strength declined with age. The *Family Doctor* revealed in 1910 that lifting power decreased by 2 per cent between the ages of thirty and forty, and by a further 8 per cent between the ages of forty and fifty.[5] The *British Medical Journal* reported in 1973 that a study of cross-country runners and skiers showed that there was 'a decrease of 5–10% in the performance every 10 years from optimum age for the event'.[6] It has also

4. W. G. Hopkins and N. P. Walker, 'The Meaning of "Physical Fitness"', *Preventive Medicine*, 17, 1988, pp. 764–73. Also J. A. Muir Gray, 'Health Beliefs and Attitudes as they Affect Preventive Practices and Self-care', *Ageing International*, Autumn, 1983, p. 8.
5. *Family Doctor*, 17 September 1910.
6. L. E. Böttiger, 'Regular Decline in Physical Working Capacity with Age', *British Medical Journal*, 4 August 1973. Also *The Times*, 7 September 1935; R. M. Belbin, 'Middle Age: What Happens to Ability?', in R. Owen (ed.), *Middle Age*, BBC, 1967, p. 100.

been known that physical dexterity began to decline from about
the age of thirty. As a *British Medical Journal* leader explained in
1950, 'the conclusion seems to be that the ability to make rapid
and accurate movements and to keep on making them declines
steeply in early middle age'.[7] It has been found time and time again
that visual efficiency too began to decline in early middle age. 'The
age when spectacles become a necessity varies much', admitted the
Family Doctor in 1890, 'but with eyes normal and well matched in
early life it may be expected about the age of forty-five'.[8] A hundred
years later, the Carnegie Inquiry into the Third Age agreed that
some forms of decline were inevitable and irreversible.

> Static visual activity is the ability to resolve fine spatial detail and
> declines from around 45 years of age ...
> The visual field, the extent of sight when fixating forward, is main-
> tained until the age of 35 years and declines slightly between the ages
> of 40 and 50 and thereafter at a progressively faster rate.[9]

It is known too that the middle aged were more vulnerable than
young adults to a long and alarming list of diseases. They were
more likely to suffer from eye diseases like glaucoma, digestive disorders like duodenal ulcers and gallstones, respiratory illnesses like
bronchitis, pneumonia and lung cancer, and cardio-vascular complications such as angina, varicose veins, high blood pressure and
coronary artery disease.[10] In fact, even if those in their forties and
fifties were fortunate enough to avoid such threats to their well-
being, there were others to which they were almost certain to suc-
cumb. 'By middle age', they were warned in 1976, 'there is bound
to be some degree of osteoarthritis'.[11] As a survey carried out in
1988 revealed, those aged between 45 and 54 were twice as likely
as those ten years younger to suffer from a disability such as
osteoarthritis of the knee.[12]

7. *British Medical Journal*, 8 April 1950.
8. *Family Doctor*, 7 June 1890. Also *Woman's Way*, 18 January 1930.
9. Carnegie Inquiry into the Third Age, *Health: Abilities and Wellbeing in the Third Age*, Carnegie Trust, 1992, p. 31. Also A. Heron, 'Psychological Changes with Age: The Present Status of Research', in W. B. Yapp and G. H. Bourne (eds), *The Biology of Ageing*, Institute of Biology, London 1957, pp. 92–3; *Daily Mail*, 4 May 1960.
10. *Family Doctor*, 26 March, 23 July 1910; *Lancet*, 17 January 1976; Consumers' Association, *Middle Age*, pp. 58–69; R. F. L. Logan, 'Health Hazards: I The Size and Nature of the Risks', in Owen (ed.), *Middle Age*, pp. 74–7; Carnegie Inquiry, *Health*, p. 32.
11. Consumers' Association, *Middle Age*, p. 25.
12. Carnegie Inquiry, *Health*, p. 52. Also B. D. Cox *et al.*, *The Health and Lifestyle Survey*, Health Promotion Research Trust, Hampton, 1987.

Gradually, the medical profession began to recognise its need to learn more about middle age. In 1918, the Medical Officer of Health for Peterborough suggested a survey of the middle aged in order to detect early signs of disease.[13] In 1948, it was reported that doctors were investigating the possibility that it was the strain of the war – and not the strain of ageing – that was turning people's hair grey.[14] However, it was not until the 1960s and 1970s that the study of 'Disabilities in Middle Age' seemed finally to acquire some academic respectability.[15] Indeed, it is striking that in 1976 the *British Medical Journal* chose ignorance about middle age to challenge what it saw as the complacency of the profession.

> The content of an average *British Medical Journal* might suggest that the remaining gaps in medical knowledge are interstices in the small print, but the falseness of this view was plainly shown last week at the symposium on medical problems of middle-aged women organised jointly, by the BMA and the Royal College of Obstetricians and Gynaecologists.[16]

There is no denying either that the mid-life decline in physical capacity and resistance to disease was matched by a certain deterioration in intellectual ability. It can be shown without too much difficulty that age brought with it some decline in such basic intellectual skills as memory, attention and speed of reaction. Long-term memory grew less reliable, the ability to ignore irrelevant detail proved more difficult, and reaction times when undertaking complex tasks became appreciably longer.[17]

However, it is much more difficult to show whether, and to what extent, age brought with it a decline in more fundamental – and more important – attributes, such as intelligence and creativity. Intelligence, of course, is notoriously difficult to define and to measure. Indeed, the older the subject, the more difficult it is to measure his/her intelligence. This is because intelligence is usually measured by intelligence tests, and practising the tests can help to improve performance. 'As middle-aged people are less conversant with them than younger adults so it would follow that the true

13. *Lancet*, 1 May 1920.   14. *Sunday Graphic*, 5 December 1948.
15. *British Medical Journal*, 18 November 1967.
16. *British Medical Journal*, 24 July 1976.
17. *Lancet*, 12 August 1961; A. T. Welford, 'On Changes of Performance with Age', *Lancet*, 17 February 1962; Carnegie Inquiry, *Health*, pp. 16–17; Heron, 'Psychological Changes', pp. 94–7; A. P. Thompson, 'Problems of Ageing and Chronic Sickness', *British Medical Journal*, 6 August 1949.

scores of middle-aged adults may be under-represented.'[18] Of course, such under-representation can be allowed for, but even when this is done it appears that the lower scores recorded by the middle aged can be explained neither by unfamiliarity with the tests nor by the ways in which they are conducted. We must accept, it seems, 'that "intelligence" does show a downward trend by the forties on average in most of the studies that have been reported'.[19]

It was accepted for many years that creativity too declined with age. As Sir William Osler famously announced at the beginning of the century,

> The effective, moving, vitalising work of the world is done between the ages of twenty-five and forty – these golden years of plenty, the anabolic or constructive period, in which there is always a balance in the mental bank and the credit is still good.[20]

Fortunately, the relationship between age and creativity, like that between age and intelligence, has now received a good deal of serious attention. Unfortunately, this attention has tended to focus upon the creativity of an elite, a group which because of its achievements in a variety of scientific, cultural and intellectual pursuits was quite untypical of the population as a whole. Nevertheless, the research that has been carried out since the 1950s draws an important distinction between the quantity and the quality of creative achievement. H. C. Lehman found that in England (as in Russia, Italy, France, Germany and the United States), 'the peak period of output came in the thirties in fourteen of the sixteen fields studied. The forties became the second most productive age, but the fifties, were less than half as productive as the thirties.' However,

> Taking the criterion of people's best work Lehman found that the peak period came earlier than the most productive period usually by half a decade, but sometimes by rather more. For example, in literature the most productive period is in the age group 40–44 but the peak period for an author's most outstanding work is much earlier at 25–29.[21]

18. Belbin, 'Middle Age', p. 103. Also W. Hobson, 'Functional Changes with Age in Relation to the Employment of the Elderly', in Yapp and Bourne (eds), *Ageing*, pp. 76–7.

19. Belbin, 'Middle Age', p. 103. Also Horn and Donaldson, 'Intellectual Decline', p. 718.

20. Cited *Lancet*, 4 August 1951.

21. Belbin, 'Middle Age', p. 103. Also E. Jacques, 'The Mid-life Crisis', in Owen (ed.), *Middle Age*, pp. 22–30.

When Betty Friedan reviewed the literature on age and creativity in 1994, she uncovered an 'age curve' that was both rather more complicated and, no doubt, rather more acceptable to those in their middle and later years.

> The peak around the late twenties or early thirties with steep descents thereafter was found in pure mathematics and theoretical physics. In other fields – novel writing, history, philosophy, medicine, general scholarship (and statesmanship) – a more gradual rise to the fifties was found, with a minimal if not entirely absent drop-off thereafter.[22]

In so far as middle age saw changes in intellectual ability and physical capacity, they were matched, to a certain extent, by changes in psychological well-being. This, however, is an exceptionally complicated area with which to deal. If it is difficult to distinguish between the physiological, psychological, environmental, economic and social causes of physical well-being, it sometimes seems almost impossible to identify and isolate the complex origins of psychological health and ill-health.

Sexuality is a case in point. It is easy enough to point out that sexual interest and activity tended to decline in middle age. 'From adolescence onwards', claimed a Belgian researcher in 1979, 'there is a continuous decline in [male] sexual interest, arousal and activity, without a sudden discontinuity in any age group.'

> If the frequency of orgasm is taken as a parameter . . . it is found that at age 50 frequency has fallen to about 50% of what it was at age 30. . . . An even more dramatic decline with age may be observed in the capacity for repeated orgasm. This reaches its peak in pre-adolescence, declining very rapidly after 20 years of age. . . . The quality of sexual activity also decreases with age. . . . Frequency of erectal impotence increases exponentially with age: at 40, 50, 60 and 75 years respectively, about 2, 7, 28 and 50% of males are affected.[23]

It is a great deal more difficult to explain these, and the other changes in sexuality that occurred during middle age. This, of course, is not in the least surprising, given that sexual attitudes, like sexual behaviour, have always been shrouded in secrecy and clouded by conjecture. It is clear, however, that the roots of middle-aged sexuality, like those of other age groups, were social as well as economic,

22. B. Friedan, *The Fountain of Age*, Vintage, 1994, p. 575. Also pp. 88–90; A. Irwin, 'Life Can Begin at Forty', *Times Higher Education Supplement*, 9 September 1994.
23. A. Vermeulen, 'Decline in Sexual Activity in Ageing Men: Correlation with Sex Hormone Levels and Testicular Changes', *Journal of Biosocial Science Supplement*, 6, 1979, p. 5. Also *Woman*, 14 September 1985.

psychological as well as physiological. 'Undoubtedly, physiological changes do alter sexual capacities in later life', conceded J. and C. D. Hendricks, 'yet their influence is vastly exaggerated. Psychological elements are probably far more consequential in determining the character of older people's sex lives.'[24] Alex Comfort explained the situation with some style:

> old folks stop having sex for the same reasons they stop riding a bicycle – general infirmity, thinking it looks ridiculous, no bicycle – and of these reasons the greatest is the social image of the dirty old man and the asexual, undesirable older woman.[25]

It seems then that some generalisation is now possible. For however difficult it may be to disentangle the roots of middle-aged sexuality, there seems to be general agreement that both sexual interest and sexual activity tended to decline in middle age. It was a decline which, it is agreed, often had significant psychological origins and significant psychological consequences, most obviously perhaps in the guise of depressive illness.

In fact, the study of depression provides a further illustration of the difficulty of distinguishing between the psychological, physiological and other causes of health and ill-health.[26] It has frequently been suggested that depressive illnesses became more common in middle age, as those in their forties and fifties struggled to adapt to their physical, intellectual – and sexual – decline. As the *Lancet* argued in 1913, 'It is only to be expected that failing sight, failing hearing, diminished muscular activity, and the many other defects of increasing age should bring to those who come to be aware of them regrets or even repining'.[27] As Mike Featherstone and Mike Hepworth pointed out in 1982,

> Generally speaking people tend to think less of themselves as they grow older and this is not due simply to the frailties of old age. A variety of studies show that changes in face and figure reflected in the mirror and the reactions of day-to-day contacts have an important part to play. Confrontation with the stereotypes of ageing can therefore produce feelings of anxiety, depression and desperation

24. J. Hendricks and C. D. Hendricks, 'Sexuality in Later Life', in V. Carver and P. Liddiard (eds), *An Ageing Population: A Reader and Sourcebook*, Hodder and Stoughton, 1978, p. 64.

25. Cited Hendricks and Hendricks, 'Sexuality', p. 65.

26. J. Mirowsky and C. E. Ross, 'Age and Depression', *Journal of Health and Social Behaviour*, 33, 1992, pp. 187–205.

27. *Lancet*, 17 May 1913.

during the middle years when the sense of time running out first takes root.[28]

These feelings of anxiety, depression and desperation could lead not only to personal misery but also to marital discord, family break-up and, in extreme cases, attempts at suicide.[29] Suicide, of course, is a dauntingly complex subject to try to analyse historically. Attempting suicide was not the same as committing suicide. Attempting suicide was defined as a crime before but not after 1961, and even following decriminalisation it seems certain that a substantial, albeit unknown, proportion of suicides continued to be recorded as accidental deaths.[30] Nonetheless, Figure 3.1 is most revealing. It shows that both before and after decriminalisation suicide rates were considerably higher among the middle aged than among adolescents; it suggests, in other words, that in so far as suicide was a measure of depression, the middle aged were more prone to depressive illness than the young.[31]

What then was the relationship between age and health? To what extent were popular views about middle-aged deterioration borne out in practice? It seems incontrovertible from the evidence produced so far that middle age did see some decline in physical capacity, intellectual capacity and psychological well-being. However, it is a decline that is frustratingly difficult to encapsulate, let alone to quantify, with any sort of precision.

The most promising approach is to compare the mortality of the middle aged with the mortality of those in young adulthood. Of course, such a procedure is by no means ideal. One obvious difficulty is that mortality is not necessarily an accurate guide to morbidity: it was possible after all to live a short but healthy life, or a long but unhealthy one. Another difficulty is that the form in which mortality data are usually presented (for ages 25–34, 35–44, 45–54 and so on) makes them inconvenient to use when it has been decided to define middle age as the years between the ages of 40 and 59. Nevertheless, the comparisons that can be made – between some of the

28. Hepworth and Featherstone, *Middle Age*, p. 13. Also Sir J. Richardson cited in *British Medical Journal*, 18 November 1967; Friedan, *Fountain of Age*, p. 118; Mirowsky and Ross, 'Age'.

29. F. Post, 'Personality in Later Middle Age', in Owen (ed.), *Middle Age*, pp. 51–2; G. Greer, *The Change; Women, Ageing and the Menopause*, Penguin, 1992, p. 107.

30. C. A. H. Watts to *British Medical Journal*, 5 July 1975; *British Medical Journal*, 23 July 1977.

31. D. Lester to *British Medical Journal*, 9 December 1972; B. M. Barraclough to *British Medical Journal*, 3 February 1973. Cf. K. Hill, *The Long Sleep: Young People and Suicide*, Virago, 1995.

middle aged and some of those in young adulthood – are most telling. Thus Figure 3.2 reveals that the mortality rates of those aged
between 45 and 54 were between two and six times higher than of
those aged between 25 and 34. Faced with such findings, it seems
difficult to do other than accept the validity of popular views about
the deterioration of health during middle age.

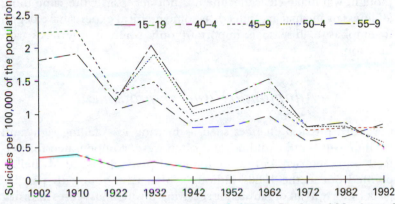

Sources: *Annual Report of the Registrar General of Births, Deaths and Marriages of
England and Wales*, 1902, 1910; *Registrar General's Statistical Review of England
and Wales*, 1922–72; Office of Population Censuses and Surveys, *Mortality
Statistics: Cause*, 1982–92.

Figure 3.1   *Middle-aged and adolescent suicide rates, 1902–92*

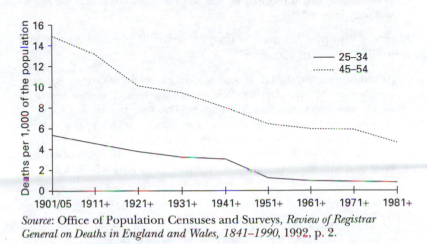

Source: Office of Population Censuses and Surveys, *Review of Registrar
General on Deaths in England and Wales, 1841–1990*, 1992, p. 2.

Figure 3.2   *Middle-aged and young adult mortality, 1901/05–81/85*

Nonetheless, such views still need to be approached with a good deal of caution. It remains all too easy to oversimplify, and so misunderstand, the nature of the relationship between age and health. It is tempting, but mistaken, to regard the decline which took place in middle-aged health as both universal and substantial. In fact, when the decline was universal, it was rarely substantial; and when it was substantial, it was rarely universal. Moreover, as a moment's thought will make clear, decline was not necessarily the same thing as illness or incapacity. Indeed, as some medical experts have begun to emphasise, disease is important only when it interferes with function.[32]

Adaptability and improvement

Certainly, physical changes such as hearing loss, failing sight and declining strength could be, and often were, compensated for perfectly satisfactorily. As the occupational psychologist R. M. Belbin pointed out in the 1960s, although 'Man is undoubtedly past his peak by forty as an organism for receiving through his senses information about his environment', this deterioration was far less of a problem than it appeared at first sight.

> Thousands of years ago, and to a lesser extent even a century ago, this must have been a serious limitation in his everyday activities. The impact nowadays is relatively slight. A person engaged in competitive sport might feel that he had lost his 'eye', but others are not seriously affected.[33]

Man was also past his peak at forty in terms of physical energy and muscular strength. However,

> As with the senses, the fall in muscle strength seems of only marginal significance in everyday life. Few situations present themselves in which maximum exertion is required. The car, the labour saving devices in the household, mechanical handling in the factory and many other instances of the replacement of manpower by horsepower have transformed the demands of work, the normal drudgery of existence and with them the physical effects of becoming middle-aged.[34]

32. Cited Friedan, *Fountain of Age*, p. 388. Also Maurice Wiggin in *Sunday Graphic*, 5 February 1950.
33. Belbin, 'Middle Age', p. 99.
34. Belbin, 'Middle Age', p. 99. Also Böttiger, 'Regular Decline'.

There were ways too of compensating for the intellectual failings and psychological difficulties that manifested themselves in middle age.[35] Experience, flexibility and the adoption of coping strategies – from making lists to avoiding stressful situations – could make up for many, if not most, of the difficulties that were encountered.[36] 'It cannot be overstressed', the middle aged were reassured, 'that the great majority of ageing people change little, and . . . show excellent adaption to the special demands and restrictions of middle and late life.'[37]

In fact, it is a great deal more difficult to generalise about the relationship between age and health (and between age, health and individual responsibility) than many existing studies – and much of the foregoing discussion – might lead one to suppose. Accordingly, it is the purpose of the remainder of this chapter to explore some of the more important barriers to generalisation about middle-aged health. It will be shown that the health of the middle aged improved during the course of the twentieth century, and that differences in middle-aged health owed less to individual factors like personality and attitude than to impersonal – and uncontrollable – factors such as gender and class. Indeed, it will be suggested that with gender differences growing wider in middle age, the years between forty and sixty tended to see a divergence, rather than a convergence, in physical, intellectual and emotional well-being.[38]

It can be shown quite readily that the health of the middle aged improved – and improved substantially – during the course of the century. So while it is true that some threats to middle-aged health persisted or intensified, many of the more serious conditions became less common and/or less severe. So, contrary to a good deal of popular opinion,[39] the middle aged shared in the more general improvement in health standards that was enjoyed by the population as a whole.

It must be conceded that some threats to the well-being of the middle aged continued virtually unchecked. This was because the medical advances which did so much to transform the life chances of those in the developed world were at their most effective in

35. *British Medical Journal*, 9 May 1953.
36. Friedan, *Fountain of Age*, pp. 86, 203.   37. Post, 'Personality', p. 52.
38. *Lancet*, 2 December 1905, 24 October 1953; *Family Doctor*, 17 September 1910; Friedan, *Fountain of Age*, pp. 40, 425.
39. Consumers' Association, *Middle Age*, p. 57; A. Eyton, *The F-Plan*, Penguin, 1982, p. 71.

dealing with the dangers of childhood and adolescence.[40] The result, as one commentator on middle-age health has pointed out, was that accidents, strokes and bronchities continued to act as the 'three corporals of death'. 'In middle and later years with a lifetime of wear and tear on ageing tissues and with mixed virus infections, even the latest fashionable antibiotics are not a "wonder cure".'[41]

It is more difficult to comment with confidence upon long-term trends in the psychological health – and ill-health – of the middle aged. The evidence is fragmentary and inconsistent, and the interpretation of longitudinal data is always fraught with particular difficulty: the diagnosis of depression and other psychological illnesses varied according both to medical fashion and to the prevailing economic and political orthodoxy. It seems, however, that although each generation believed it faced new threats to its well-being,[42] the psychological health of the middle aged probably continued relatively unchanged. 'It is difficult to interpret statistics collected over the last one hundred years', admitted a 1960s study of 'personality in middle age', 'but there is very little evidence to suggest that there has been an increase of mental or nervous illhealth among the elderly.'[43]

It must be conceded of course that some threats to the physical health of the middle aged became more serious during the course of the century. 'The increased survival rates of susceptibles who formerly would have been lost in infancy or childhood, coupled with the new diet, produced a new pattern of disease and disability that has persisted to the present, where coronary disease, cardiac disease, cancer and hypertension comprise the four leading reported causes of death.'[44] This new pattern of disease and disability struck hard at the middle aged. The president of the General Medical Council warned the House of Lords in 1968 that,

> The most difficult tasks which confront health education are those which apply to adults in middle age, when the aim of health education

40. K. McPherson and D. Coleman, 'Health', in A. H. Halsey (ed.), *British Social Trends since 1900: A Guide to the Changing Social Structure of Britain*, Macmillan, Basingstoke, 1988, p. 418.

41. Logan, 'Health Hazards', p. 80. Also p. 81.

42. For example, *Family Doctor*, 16 April 1910.

43. Post, 'Personality', p. 52. Also Logan, 'Health Hazards', p. 81. Figure 3.1 shows, of course, a substantial decline in middle-aged suicide during the course of the century.

44. F. B. Smith, 'Health', in J. Benson (ed.), *The Working Class in England 1875–1914*, Croom Helm, 1984, p. 52.

is to modify deleterious habits – cigarette smoking, over-indulgence in alcohol, over-eating, lack of exercise, and the like.[45]

However, this catalogue of self-indulgence must not be allowed to obscure the fact that the middle aged were becoming more, rather than less, healthy. For it is a fundamental paradox of the relationship between age and health that the new twentieth-century pattern of disease and disability advantaged as well as disadvantaged those in their middle years. As an editorial in the *Lancet* explained in 1953, 'since the forces tending to keep us alive are to a large extent the same as those operating to keep us well, many of us will feel fitter than did aged people in the past'.[46]

Once again, it is difficult to capture the middle-age experience of health. Once again, however, the most obvious approach is to examine the age-specific mortality statistics which are available. It will be recalled that Figure 3.2 (see page 45) compared the mortality rates of the middle aged and young adults, showing that the former were considerably higher than the latter. It shows too that the death rate of those aged between 45 and 54 fell by more than a half between the beginning and middle of the century, and continued to fall, though more slowly, between the early 1950s and the early 1980s.

The other obvious way of attempting to capture the middle-age experience of health is to compare the expectation of life of those turning forty at various dates during the course of the century. Figure 3.3 reveals that, as might be expected, the number of years that a forty-year-old man or woman could expect to live increased substantially – by more than a third – between 1901 and 1991.

Here then are two key indicators of middle-aged health. Although neither mortality not life expectancy constitutes an ideal measure of health and ill-health, together they provide a most valuable guide to changing standards of middle-aged health. They point to a clear and substantial, albeit apparently easily overlooked, improvement in the well-being of those in their forties and fifties. It is an improvement that must no longer be ignored.

Here then is one reason why it is so difficult to generalise about the health of the middle aged. It would be utterly unrealistic to attempt to discuss the relationship between age and health (and between age, health and individual responsibility) as though it

45. *British Medical Journal*, 6 January 1968. Also Smith, 'Health', p. 52; Logan, 'Health Hazards', p. 74; Carnegie Inquiry, *Health*, p. 73.
46. *Lancet*, 24 October 1953.

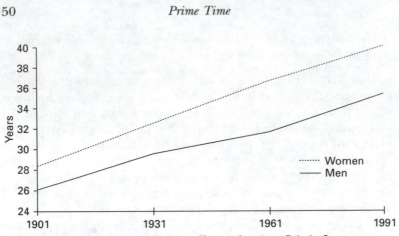

Source: H. Jones, *Health and Society in Twentieth-century Britain*, Longman, 1994, p. 196.

Figure 3.3   *Expectation of life at forty, 1901–91*

remained unchanged in the face of the massive economic, social, cultural and political changes that have taken place over the past hundred years.

Gender, age and health

Another reason for caution when generalising about the relationship between age and health (and especially about the relationship between age, decline and individual responsibility) is that men's and women's experiences tended to diverge in middle age. There were differences at all ages of course, but they became considerably greater between the ages of forty and sixty. For as women knew only too well, and as men were only too keen to point out, middle age meant the menopause – and the menopause, many believed, meant that women became tired, depressed and difficult to deal with.[47] It would be as unrealistic to discuss the relationship between middle age and health without considering differences between the sexes as it would be to do so without paying attention to changes over the course of time.

However, it is important not to accept uncritically the emphasis that many commentators placed upon the menopause, and thus

47. C. Bruck, 'Menopause', *Human Behaviour*, 8, 1979; K. I. MacPherson, 'Menopause as Disease: The Social Construction of a Metaphor', *Advances in Nursing Science*, 3, 1981.

exaggerate the gap that developed in middle age between male and female standards of health. It has been seen, after all, that the middle aged of both sexes underwent a broadly similar set of physical, intellectual and psychological changes. Both men and women lost muscular strength, became more prone to disease, and needed to cope with sensory decline and the fact that they were likely to be less active sexually than they had been earlier in life. Yet these were changes brought about by age, not by the menopause; these were changes with which both men and women had to contend.

It has been seen too that there were commentators who, while accepting the importance of the menopause, claimed that it did not widen the gap between men and women in the way, and to the extent, that was usually suggested. Men, they believed, underwent their own version of the menopause.[48] Such claims need to be approached with a healthy dose of scepticism, but clearly the existence of a male menopause (or anything like it) would have the effect of narrowing the gap between men and women in middle age.

The gap is certainly narrowed by the fact that a surprisingly large number of women experienced few, if any, of the health problems that are commonly associated with the menopause. The statistical evidence, patchy and partial though it is, suggests that the association between menopause and ill-health was sometimes more apparent than real. A survey of 1,200 London teachers carried out between 1926 and 1932 revealed that 15 per cent of the sample reported no menopausal symptoms at all, and that only 10 per cent reported being so incapacitated that they had to take to their beds or stay away from work. It was not what the *Lancet* had expected.

> In view of the general impression acquired from the literature on the subject, it was somewhat surprising to find that approximately 900 out of 1,000 unselected women stated that that they had carried on their daily routine without a single interruption due to menopausal symptoms.[49]

Gradually, such findings began to be publicised and replicated. By the late 1950s, for instance, women's magazines were reassuring their readers that fully 50 per cent of menopausal women suffered

48. See, for example, M. Featherstone and M. Hepworth, 'The History of the Male Menopause 1848–1936', *Maturitas*, 7, 1985; *British Medical Journal*, 13 December 1930, 9 May 1953; M. Carruthers, *Male Menopause: Restoring Vitality and Virility*, HarperCollins, 1995.

49. *Lancet*, 14 January 1933. Also 23 October 1943; *British Medical Journal*, 30 January 1915, 13 December 1930; L. Fairfield, 'An Address on the Health of Professional Women', *Lancet*, 3 July 1926; Bruck, 'Menopause', p. 41.

no physical symptoms other than the ending of their periods.[50] In
1980, an investigation carried out in Glasgow concluded that the
menopause was less important than personality and environment
in accounting for the physical and psychological difficulties experienced by middle-aged women.[51]

The fact that many women avoided the terrors of the menopause does not of course invalidate the claim that middle age saw
a significant divergence in men's and women's physical and psychological well-being. For no matter how much effort is devoted to identifying a male menopause or correcting popular misconceptions
about the female menopause, middle-aged women had to deal with
problems that middle-aged men did not. They had to cope not
only with unwanted physical and emotional changes which men were
spared, but also with unpleasant and unwarranted assumptions about
their physical resilience and emotional stability.

It is these deep-seated assumptions about the menopause and its
consequences that make it so difficult to assess women's physical
and psychological well-being in middle age. Indeed, as feminist historians have been at pains to point out, the menopause was socially
constructed: it was discovered by male doctors, defined by them as
a disease, and treated by them as a medical condition.[52] Hysterectomy
was a popular treatment in the 1950s and 1960s, a procedure which
magazines like *Woman's Realm* were happy to endorse. 'You can
often be a better wife in every way after the surgical removal of
symptoms which made you feel permanently tired and irritable and
out of sorts.'[53] Hormone replacement therapy became fashionable
from the mid 1970s onwards, with Margaret Thatcher supposedly
leading the way. As Virginia Ironside reassured the readers of *Woman*
in 1985, 'Hormones are hardly "drugs" in the way you regard them.
All you will be doing is replacing hormones that used to exist in
your body naturally with ones given by your doctor.'[54]

50. *Woman*, 18 October 1958; *Woman's Realm*, 2 January 1960. Also A. Sharman,
The Middle Years: The Change of Life, Livingstone, 1962, chs 3–4.
51. J. G. Grene and D. J. Cooke, 'Life Stress and Symptoms at the Climacterium',
British Journal of Psychiatry, 136, 1980, pp. 486–91. Also *Lancet*, 23 October 1943, 17
July 1982; *British Medical Journal*, 30 January 1960; Bruck, 'Menopause', p. 44.
52. Greer, *The Change*, pp. 13, 105; MacPherson, 'Menopause'; P. A. Kaufert,
'Myth and the Menopause', *Sociology of Health and Illness*, 4, 1982; S. Coney, *The Menopause Industry*, Penguin, 1991.
53. *Woman's Realm*, 30 January 1960. Also *Woman*, 5 March 1960; Consumers'
Association, *Middle Age*, p. 93.
54. *Woman*, 27 July 1985. Also *British Medical Journal*, 30 January 1960, 30 June
1973, 28 September 1974, 3 April 1976, 23 July 1977; *Lancet*, 7 June 1975, 26 May
1979, 17 July 1982; *Woman's Own*, 2 January 1995.

It is no easy task to penetrate such deeply held professional and popular beliefs about the menopause, its causes and its consequences. Nonetheless, the analysis of these beliefs is central to any assessment of the health of middle-aged women. The conclusion must be that it was the combination of social stigmatisation, psychological adjustment and physical decline that undermined the health of middle-aged women, and so widened the gap between them and their male contemporaries.

Whatever the reasons, it seems undeniable that differences in the physical health of men and women grew more pronounced in middle age. Men were more prone than women to glaucoma, ulcers and prostate problems, and four to five times more liable to suffer from bronchitis, lung cancer and coronary heart disease.[55] Women were more likely to experience difficulties such as osteoporosis, gall stones, breast cancer and urinary incontinence.[56] A large-scale survey carried out in the late 1980s confirmed that middle-aged women were rather more likely than middle-aged men to be chronically ill, and a great deal more likely to report symptoms such as feeling tired, finding it difficult to sleep and 'worrying over every little thing'.[57]

It was women, not men, who endured excessively heavy periods, ceased menstruating and suffered from night sweats and hot flushes. Indeed, even the most unsparing critics of the stigmatisation of middle-aged women concede that hot flushes were common, and could be distressing and embarrassing. Germaine Greer explains, for example, that hot flushes 'are experienced by anything from 61 per cent to 75 per cent of all women at menopause'.[58] Connie Bruck cites a survey of 638 45–54-year-old London women.

> Of hot flushes, night sweats, headache, dizzy spells, palpitations, sleeplessness, depression and weight gain, only the hot flush (sometimes associated with night sweats) showed a distinct relationship to the menopause, with four out of five menopausal women experiencing them.[59]

It is a great deal more difficult to decide whether, and to what extent, the psychological differences between men and women grew

---

55. *Lancet*, 17 January 1976; Logan, 'Health Hazards', pp. 72–3; Friedan, *Fountain of Age*, p. 117.
56. Consumers' Association, *Middle Age*, pp. 25, 69; Carnegie Inquiry, *Health*, p. 59.
57. Cox, et al., *Health and Lifestyle*, pp. 9, 61.   58. Greer, *The Change*, p. 112.
59. Bruck, 'Menopause', p. 44. Also Open University, *Birth to Old Age: Health in Transition*, Open University Press, Milton Keynes, 1985, p. 149.

more pronounced in middle age. Any attempt to analyse the psychological health and ill-health of the middle aged is complicated – and compromised – by the stigmatisation of the menopausal woman. This stigmatisation makes it difficult, and often impossible, to distinguish at all satisfactorily between women's psychological well-being and society's views of that well-being. It seems, however, that psychologically, as well as physiologically, the experiences of men and women did tend to diverge in middle age. The examination of such indicators of emotional ill-health as sexual difficulty, depression, certain sorts of crime and suicide suggests that men and women reacted differently – and more differently than young adults – to the circumstances in which they found themselves.

The relationship between age, gender and sexuality has received surprisingly little serious attention, although it is often suggested that both men and women were likely to experience sexual difficulties in middle age.[60] The relationship between age, gender and depression has attracted a great deal more attention. Some commentators ascribed the depression of middle-aged women to physiological change, others to individual personality, and others again to family circumstances or the nature of contemporary society.[61] In 1910, the *Family Doctor* blamed the tendency of middle-aged women to become depressed on the boredom of housework: 'Women at home often get low-spirited, fretful, dejected and sometimes even cross. And they lose their good looks, and become old before their time.'[62]

> To the ordinary woman of poetic tendencies, but no definite inclination towards the dramatic side of life, thirty-five is an age which cannot fail to bring with it a feeling of melancholy and dissatisfaction. . . . Partners at balls are less persistent, and fewer in number.[63]

Sixty years later, it was more common to attribute the depression of middle-aged women to the difficulties they experienced in dealing with their elderly parents and teenage children. 'Women who have overprotective or involved relationships with their children are more

60. Consumers' Association, *Middle Age*, pp. 108–11; Vermeulen, 'Decline'; *Mail on Sunday*, 8 October 1995.

61. *British Medical Journal*, 30 January 1960, 9 August 1975, 15 May 1976, 24 July 1976.

62. *Family Doctor*, 15 October 1910. Also *Lancet*, 23 October 1943; P. Warren and G. Parry, 'Paid Employment and Women's Psychological Well-being', *Psychological Bulletin*, 91, 1982, pp. 498–516.

63. *Family Doctor*, 22 October 1910.

likely to suffer depression in their postparental period than women who do not have such relationships.'[64] The *Lancet* took rather a different line, attributing some at least of the psychiatric and psychosexual problems of middle age to contemporary 'attitudes in our society, with its emphasis on the importance of youth and sexual attractiveness'.[65]

However, nearly all commentators seemed to agree upon one thing. Whatever their personal background, disciplinary specialism or ideological presuppositions, all believed that middle-aged women were more vulnerable than younger women and men of the same age to the corrosive effects of depressive illness. The *Lancet* reported in 1910 that although 'many women retain an unimpaired cheerfulness and sweetness of disposition' during the menopause, 'the nervous symptoms most frequently met with are irritability and mental depression'.[66] In 1975, the *British Medical Journal* carried a study which concluded with the observation that whatever the relationship between morbidity and the menopause, there was no doubt that minor psychiatric illnesses were common among middle-aged women.[67] Such women, it was generally agreed, were more likely than younger women and men of the same age to suffer from some form of depressive illness.

The relationship between age, gender and certain types of crime has also attracted some attention. It appears at first sight that popular stereotyping was probably correct in suggesting that middle-aged women were more likely than other groups to indulge in petty crimes such as shoplifting.[68] However, the relationship was more complicated than such views allow. Although detailed evidence is available only for the second half of the century, it seems to undermine the conventional image of the menopausal shoplifter. When allowance is made for the shopping habits of different groups of the population, it transpires that the middle aged stole no more than any other age group, and that while there were more female

64. P. B. Bart, 'Depression in Middle-aged Women', in V. Gornick and B. K. Moran (eds), *Woman in Sexist Society: Studies in Power and Powerlessness*, Basic Books, London, 1971, p. 177, Also *British Medical Journal*, 18 March 1967, 9 August 1975.

65. *British Medical Journal*, 24 July 1976.

66. A. E. Giles to *Lancet*, 12 February 1910.

67. C. B. Ballinger, 'Psychiatric Morbidity and the Menopause: Screening of General Population Sample', *British Medical Journal*, 9 August 1975. Also C. B. Ballinger, 'Psychiatric Morbidity and the Menopause: Clinical Features', *British Medical Journal*, 15 May 1976.

68. *Sunday Graphic*, 7 July 1935.

than male shoplifters in food shops, there were more male than female shoplifters in hardware and do-it-yourself stores.[69] Nonetheless, popular stereotyping proved remarkably difficult to dislodge. When *Weekend* magazine carried a story in 1988 challenging the popular view of the shoplifter as 'a muddled, middle-aged woman or a confused pensioner', it went on to describe five 'typical cases'. Two of the five were forty-year-old women.[70]

The relationship between age, gender and suicide has also received a certain amount of attention. It was seen earlier in the chapter how difficult it is to interpret suicide data with any degree of certainty. Nonetheless, it does seem possible to draw two clear, albeit contradictory, conclusions concerning men, women and middle-aged suicide. It is known that while middle-aged women were more likely than younger women to take their own lives; Figure 3.4 reveals too that middle-aged women were less likely to do so than their male contemporaries, and that the gap tended to narrow until 1972 and to widen thereafter. These are contradictions which point yet again to the significant, and complex, ways in which men's and women's experience of health differed in middle age.

Indeed, this discussion of suicide should alert us to a broader contradiction which lies at the heart of the relationship between age, gender and health. It has been shown time and again that the health of middle-aged women was different from, and generally inferior to, that of middle-aged men. However, it must be stressed too that middle-aged women were less likely than middle-aged men to die during their forties and fifties. Figure 3.5 shows that throughout the whole of the century, the death rate of men aged 45–54 stood appreciably higher than that of women of the same age. It appears, in other words, that although middle-aged women, like women generally, were sicker than men, they were likely to outlive them. 'It would appear', Lettitia Fairfield pointed out as early as 1926, 'that in some paradoxical way women save themselves from death by becoming ill!'.[71]

It is a paradox which is central to any comparison of men's and women's health. Yet it is a paradox which reinforces rather than

69. R. Davey, 'Shoplifting: How Much Do We Know?', *Retail & Distribution Management*, 5, 1977, p. 8. Also p. 9; E. S. Abelson, *When Ladies Go A-Thieving: Middle-Class Shoplifters in the Victorian Department Store*, Oxford University Press, Oxford, 1989, p. 157.

70. *Weekend*, 3 September 1988.

71. *Lancet*, 3 July 1926. See also Jones, *Health and Society*, p. 182.

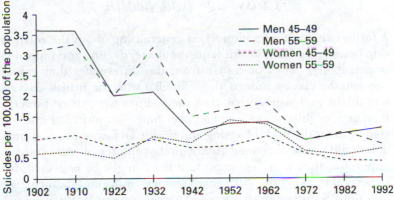

Sources: Annual Report of the Registrar General of Births, Deaths and Marriages of England and Wales, 1902, 1910; Registrar General's Statistical Review of England and Wales, 1922–72; Office of Population Censuses and Surveys, Mortality, Statistics: Cause, 1982–92.

Figure 3.4   *Middle-aged men's and women's suicide rates, 1902–92*

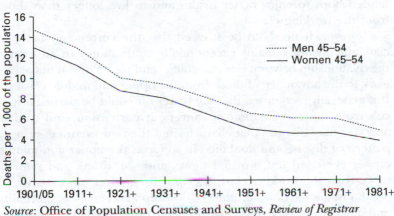

Source: Office of Population Censuses and Surveys, *Review of Registrar General on Deaths in England and Wales, 1841–1990*, 1992, p. 2.

Figure 3.5   *Middle-aged men's and women's mortality, 1901/05–81/85*

undermines the argument put forward in this chapter. For it shows yet again that there were clear differences between men's and women's experiences of health in middle age; and it suggests once again that these differences were the result less of individual personality and attitude than of more deep-seated structural factors.

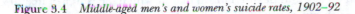

Class, age and health

A further reason for caution when generalising about the relation-ship between age and health (and about age, decline and individual responsibility) arises of course from the differences that existed between the classes. Indeed, those familiar with the British class sys-tem might well assume that class inequalities were more powerful than gender differences, changes over time – or anything else – in complicating the study of ageing and health. In fact, such an assump-tion would not be warranted. Although class differences were certainly important, they were less important than might be expected, less important than gender differences and less important than changes over time. So although class exerted a most powerful influence upon health, there is no evidence that it was more potent in middle age than at other stages of the life cycle.

Nonetheless, class remains central to any analysis of the relation-ship between age and health. For no matter which measures of health and ill-health are selected, they show that class mattered, and that as might be expected, those from the upper and middle classes tended both to enjoy better health and to live longer than those from the working class.

However, it needs to be stressed that the correlation between class and health remains exceptionally contentious. In all events, the relationship between class, morbidity and mortality did not always work to the advantage of those from the upper and middle classes.[72] It is generally recognised that the better off could be particularly at risk from the combination of cancers, hypertension, and cardiac and coronary diseases that characterised the new twentieth-century pattern of disease and disability. In so far as the upper and middle classes exercised less, worried more, and ate, drank and smoked more than the working class, they put themselves more at risk.[73]

Almost always, however, the relationship between class, morbidity and mortality worked to the disadvantage of the working class. It was discovered time, time and time again that there was a correlation between material deprivation, high morbidity and high mortality. The fact that the poor tended to do the hardest work, receive the lowest incomes, live in the least satisfactory accommodation and

---

72. Jones, *Health and Society*, pp. 172–8; McPherson and Coleman, 'Health', pp. 418–33.

73. *Family Doctor*, 22 January 1910; *Lancet*, 23 October 1943. Also A. P. Thompson to *Lancet*, 28 March 1936.

eat the least nutrititious diet meant that they also tended to suffer from the poorest health and to die at an earlier age than other social groups.[74]

In a sense, however, this is beside the point. The issue at stake is not the relationship between class and health, but the relationship between class, age and health. The issue to be addressed is not whether, and to what extent, there were class differences in health; the issue is whether, and to what extent, class differences in health became more or less pronounced during middle age.

This is a much more difficult question to answer. There is little data available, the data which does exist is not always in the form that one would wish, and the data which does exist in the form that one would wish is often extremely difficult to interpret. Accordingly, it is necessary to turn, as before, to the age-specific mortality statistics that are available on a national basis. When this is done, the result is rather surprising. For as Figure 3.6 suggests, it seems that class differences, unlike gender differences, tended to stabilise or converge, rather than diverge, during middle age.[75] The analysis of mortality rates provides no evidence at all that class differences became more pronounced in middle age.

It seems strange, it must be admitted, that the correlation between class and health did not become more pronounced in middle age. However, this lack of convergence in no way invalidates the arguments that are being put forward in this chapter. The evidence presented here on the relationship between class, age and health confirms that there were always clear differences between the middle-class and working-class experience of health; and it suggests once again that these differences were the result less of individual attitudes and lifestyle than of much more deeply entrenched inequalities in income, housing and education.[76]

It remains extremely difficult to generalise about the relationship between age and health, and especially about that between age, decline and individual responsibility. It seems, however, that while middle age saw some deterioration in physical capacity and intellectual ability, the health of those in their forties and fifties tended

74. J. Benson, *The Working Class in Britain, 1850–1939*, Longman, 1989, pp. 104, 106; R. Hoggart, *The Uses of Literacy: Aspects of Working-class Life with Special Reference to Publications and Entertainments*, Penguin, 1958, p. 46ff.; Jones, *Health and Society*, pp. 75, 173–5, 190, 198; McPherson and Coleman, 'Health', p. 421; D. Black, J. N. Norris, C. Smith and P. Townsend, *Report of the Working Group on Inequalities in Health*, Department of Health and Social Security, 1980, pp. 43, 59; Smith, 'Health', pp. 57–8.

75. Black et al., *Inequalities*, p. 60.

76. McPherson and Coleman, 'Health', p. 421; Jones, *Health and Society*, pp. 172–82.

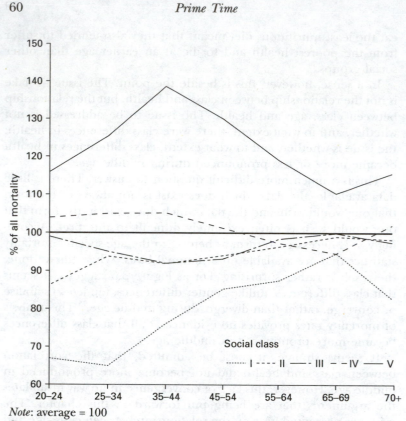

Note: average = 100
Source: *Registrar General's Decennial Supplement: Occupational Mortality, England and Wales*, 1921–61.

Figure 3.6 *Age, class and men's mortality, 1921*

both to improve and to diverge. It was a divergence that even specialists could overlook.[77] It was a divergence that was to be explained less by personality and positive thinking than by biology, genetic inheritance, gender differences and the unequal distribution of economic, social and cultural resources which will be examined in the following chapter.

77. A. T. Welford, 'On Change of Performance with Age', *Lancet*, 17 February 1962. Also review of Heron, et al., *Age and Function* in *Lancet*, 19 August 1967; Horn and Donaldson, 'Intellectual Decline', p. 701.

CHAPTER FOUR

Work, Wealth and Consumption

The material conditions of the middle aged have received far less attention than those of adolescents, young adults and the elderly – and far less too than other, more immediately arresting aspects of middle-aged life such as the menopause, the mid-life crisis and the empty-nest syndrome.[1] Such neglect is doubly unfortunate. For not only does it make it difficult to understand the day-to-day lives of the middle aged, but it also encourages those examining the more intriguing aspects of middle-aged life to overlook the possible economic basis of many of the developments and attitudes that they are considering.

Accordingly, it is the purpose of this chapter to explore the material conditions of those in their forties and fifties. It will be argued that the economic circumstances of the middle aged – like the health of the middle aged – tended both to improve and to diverge. It will be shown that the middle aged, like those from other age groups, saw their standard of living improve substantially during the course of the twentieth century, and that the middle aged, unlike those from other age groups, tended to be better off than their contemporaries at other stages of the life cycle. Indeed, it will be suggested that such improvement and advantage made the middle aged of central, albeit frequently overlooked, concern to the suppliers of an extensive, and constantly expanding, range of consumer goods and services. However, it will be shown too that such improvement, advantage and importance co-existed alongside deep-seated diversity, disadvantage and inequality. It was a dichotomy that owed less to individual attitudes and aspirations than to the

1. See, for example, J. Benson, *The Rise of Consumer Society in Britain, 1880–1980*, Longman, 1994.

fact that middle age was a period during which both gender and class differences tended to become still more pronounced than they were at earlier stages of the life cycle.

Employment, income and wealth

There is not the slightest doubt that the middle aged, like those from other age groups, saw their standard of living improve considerably during the course of the twentieth century. However, such a claim is easier to make than it is to substantiate. For it turns out to be remarkably difficult to identify the economic circumstances of the middle aged and isolate them from those of the remainder of the population.

Nonetheless, the problem is by no means insurmountable. It can certainly be shown that the income and wealth of the population as a whole grew substantially during the twentieth century, and it can be suggested with some confidence that for sixty or seventy years these changes benefited the middle aged as much as, if not more than, the rest of the population. It seems reasonable therefore to use the material conditions of the population as a whole as a convenient, albeit imperfect, guide to the material conditions of those in their middle years.

It is well known, of course, that the material circumstances of the population as a whole have been transformed since the beginning of the century. Income per person grew by 500 per cent between 1901 and 1951, and by a massive 1,300 per cent between 1951 and 1981. Even when these increases are adjusted to take account of inflation, there remained a major increase in per capita spending power. Real income per person grew by 50 per cent between 1901 and 1951, and almost doubled again between 1951 and 1981.[2] Nor was this all. The growth in real incomes was accompanied by a growth in the volume and value of assets such as property, savings, investments and pension rights. It is known, for example, that owner-occupation grew from some 10 per cent of all accommodation in 1914, to 20 per cent in 1939, 30 per cent in 1951, and more than 60 per cent by the early 1980s.[3] It is known too that this expansion of home ownership was reflected in changes in the housing

2. Benson, *Consumer Society*, p. 12; A. Dilnot, 'The Economic Environment', in A. H. Halsey (ed.), *British Social Trends since 1900: A Guide to the Changing Social Structure of Britain*, Macmillan, Basingstoke, 1988.
3. Benson, *Consumer Society*, pp. 12–13.

and other assets that were left at death. Between 1858 and 1938–39, the proportion of adults who died leaving property grew from 15 per cent to 33 per cent, and the value of their estates increased, on average, from under £2,500 to more than £3,500.[4]

There is no doubt either that during the first sixty to seventy years of the century these changes benefited the middle aged as much as, if not more than, those from other age groups. Despite the changing attitudes towards middle age that were examined in Chapter 2, there is little sign before 1970 of any increase in workplace discrimination against the middle aged or of any decline in the proportion of the middle aged who were in work.[5]

It is true that there was some increase in the volume of complaints about workplace discrimination, and that this makes it difficult to judge the incidence – as opposed to the appearance – of the disadvantages confronting the middle-aged worker. It seems clear, however, that recruitment (and no doubt training, promotion and retirement) policies varied according to prevailing economic, social and political circumstances. Nonetheless, there is surprisingly little evidence that workplace discrimination became either more common or more severe during the first half of the century. Indeed, it is telling that the individuals and groups campaigning against such discrimination in the years following the Second World War complained about the existence – but not the expansion – of discrimination in the recruitment, training, promotion and retirement of the middle aged.[6]

Sometimes, of course, employers preferred to employ those in their forties and fifties. It was seen earlier that middle age remained associated more than one might imagine with steadiness, reliability and respectability. However, this does not makes it any easier to assess the scale and significance of such positive attitudes: as might be expected, discrimination in favour of the middle aged tended to attract a good deal more attention than discrimination against them.

Certainly, some employers did discriminate in favour of those in their forties and fifties. Efforts were made to recruit the middle aged at times, and in places, of labour shortage. During the Second

4. W. D. Rubinstein, *Men of Property: The Very Wealthy in Britain since the Industrial Revolution*, Croom Helm, 1981, pp. 28–30, 32. The figures for 1858 refer to England and Wales, those for 1938–39 to Great Britain.

5. R. Slater, 'Age Discrimination', in V. Carver and P. Liddiard (eds), *An Ageing Population: A Reader and Sourcebook*, Hodder and Stoughton, 1978.

6. See, for example, *Royal Commission on Population, Report*, 1949. Cf. *Ministry of Labour Gazette*, February 1952.

World War, those unable to enlist because of age or exemption were sometimes specifically targeted.[7] During the 1980s, Tescos launched a well-publicised initiative to recruit those over fifty-five to work in three of their stores in West Sussex.[8] Efforts were made just occasionally to recruit the middle aged at times, and in places, of labour surplus. It was reported from the West Midlands in 1994 that 'Desperate job-hunters jammed a Dudley company's phone lines minutes after bosses advertised just five jobs – for the middle-aged only'. As the managing director of the company explained, 'they wanted older workers for their stability, maturity and experience': 'Written off at 40? Not with Air Movement Group you're not.'[9]

These, however, were the exceptions that proved the rule. Nearly always, employers preferred not to recruit the middle aged; nearly always, popular attitudes worked to the disadvantage, rather than the advantage, of the middle-aged worker. Whoever they were, wherever they lived, and whatever they did, the middle aged found it difficult to counter employers' perceptions of middle-aged decline, rigidity and inefficiency.[10]

Unfortunately, it is more difficult than one would imagine to chart the scale and significance of such perceptions. There are two major sets of evidence: the comments contained in interviews, autobiographies, periodicals and parliamentary papers; and the job advertisements carried in trade, local and national newspapers. But neither is easy to use and interpret. The former deals, it is true, with both overt and covert forms of discrimination and with recruitment, training, promotion and retirement, but may well exaggerate the impact of discriminatory attitudes. The latter is easier to locate and quantify, but records only overt forms of discrimination and tells us nothing at all about training, promotion and recruitment. Nonetheless, both sets of evidence point to an intriguing paradox. For although it has been seen that middle age became associated increasingly with decay and decline, it seems that the recruitment

7. *News Chronicle*, 28 May 1941. Also *Lancet*, 23 October 1943; *National Advisory Committee on the Employment of Older Men and Women, 2nd Report*, 1955, p. 8.

8. Employment Committee, Second Report, *The Employment Patterns of the Over-50s*, Volume II, 1988–89, p. 44. Also B. Friedan, *The Fountain of Age*, Vintage, 1993, p. 176.

9. Wolverhampton, *Express and Star*, 30 July 1994. Also *Sunday Times*, 12 May 1996; *The Times*, 14 May 1996; *Mail on Sunday*, 6 October 1996.

10. R. C. *Population, Report*, 1949, p. 119; *National Advisory Committee, 1st Report*, 1953, p. 13; F. Laczko and C. Phillipson, 'Defending the Right to Work: Age Discrimination in Employment', in E. McEwen (ed.), *The Unrecognised Discrimination: Views to Provoke a Debate*, Age Concern, 1990, p. 89.

of the middle aged changed little, if at all, during the first sixty or seventy years of the century.

The criticisms made about employers' attitudes changed remarkably little during the first three quarters of the century. Skilled workers complained constantly that they found it hard to obtain – and retain – employment once they had passed the age of forty. As a Birmingham engineer told the Royal Commission on the Aged Poor in 1895, 'as a man gets up, even when he gets up to fifty; if he shows grey hairs in his head, it becomes increasingly difficult for him to obtain a situation'.[11] Those in the professions also complained about the discrimination which they faced. According to a correspondent to the *Lancet* in 1907, there was an increasing tendency for public bodies to set an age limit of forty: 'Would the councillors admit that they themselves are not doing, or capable of doing, useful work in an up-to-date manner, simply because they are over 40?'[12]

These and similar criticisms continued at much the same level for the following fifty to sixty years. In the early 1930s, there were complaints that 'in the medical world 45 is the usual age limit for an appointment, an age when one could still be playing Rugby football',[13] and there was criticism that in the civil service 'we are regarded as too old at 40 for most of the public posts'. 'All honour to the young and enthusiastic, but at least some of us are middle-aged and enthusiastic, and have in addition experience which the young cannot yet have.'[14] In the late 1940s and early 1950s, there was a press campaign against the ageism of the workplace. 'Skill and experience are wasted when men and women over 40 are denied employment', protested the *Daily Sketch* in 1950. 'They are usually reliable and industrious. They are often more adaptable than those of their juniors who think they know it all already.'[15]

Nor is there much evidence to suggest that the more overt forms of discrimination were intensifying. Indeed, Figure 4.1 suggests that the proportion of job advertisements excluding those aged forty

11. *Royal Commission on the Aged Poor*, 1895, Q. 14,573, A. R. Jephcott. Also QQ. 16,576, 16,622, H. Allen; *Royal Commission on Labour*, Digest of Evidence, Group A, QQ. 23,303–4, G. Clarke; C. Booth, *Life and Labour of the People in London*, Macmillan, Basingstoke, 1892, 2nd Ser. I, pp. 88–9. 93, 97.

12. *Lancet*, 14 September 1907. Also 16 January 1904.

13. 'Juvenis' cited in *British Medical Journal*, 5 December 1931.

14. 'Ex-Temporary Civil Servant' to *Lancet*, 26 July 1930. Also 'Economy' cited in *British Medical Journal*, 12 December 1931.

15. *Daily Sketch*, 4 September 1950. Also *Lancet*, 24 October 1953; 'Work Not Want' to *Express and Star*, 13 August 1947; *Sunday Graphic*, 7 March 1948, 26 March 1950.

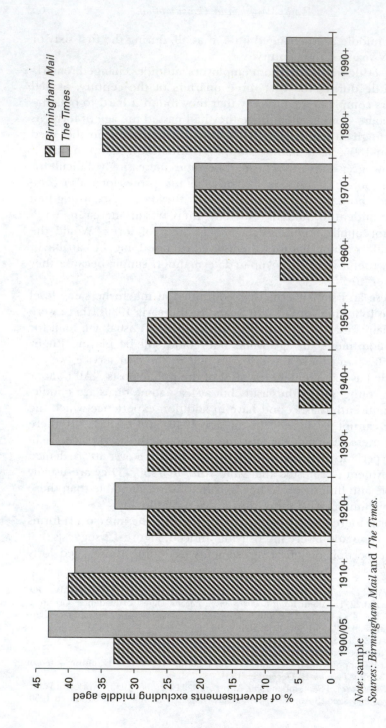

Note: sample
Sources: Birmingham Mail and The Times.

Figure 4.1 Job advertisements excluding the middle aged, 1900–90

and above declined rather than increased during the first half of the century, and declined or fluctuated thereafter depending on which newspaper carried the advertisement. One is left with the paradox that the increasing demonisation of middle age seemed to co-exist alongside the continuing employability of the middle aged. It is a paradox that is not easily resolved.

Two solutions suggest themselves. It may be perhaps that employers began to accept the view that the failings of middle age were more or less avoidable given the appropriate remedial action, and that this persuaded them to continue employing those in their forties and fifties. It seems more likely, however, that the explanation was structural rather than ideological, that although employers continued to associate middle age with decay and collapse, they believed that such failings were rendered less of an impediment by the changing nature of the labour market. As time went by, there occurred a significant decline in the importance of the physically demanding jobs for which the middle aged were – or were believed to be – fundamentally ill-equipped. It is striking, for example, that between 1911 and 1966 the proportion of the workforce engaged in manual work declined by 22 per cent, whereas the proportions employed as clerical workers and as salesmen and shop assistants increased by 131 per cent and 193 per cent respectively.[16]

It was not until the 1970s and 1980s that discrimination began to grow apace. Although Figure 4.1 suggests both an increase and a decrease in age discrimination during the second half of the century, other sources reveal how common it was to exclude the middle aged. The Department of Employment claimed in 1980 that nearly one-sixth of all vacancies filled via its job centres and employment offices were barred to those over the age of forty.[17] The Institute of Personnel Management reported in 1988 that more than one-third of all job advertisements containing age requirements specified an upper limit of forty,[18] and *Ageing International* announced in the same year that an eleven-month analysis of job openings advertised in leading national periodicals revealed that more than two-thirds of those mentioning age wished to recruit candidates who were between thirty and forty.[19]

16. A. H. Halsey, *Trends in British Society since 1900; A Guide to the Changing Social Structure of Britain*, Macmillan, Basingstoke, 1972, p. 113.

17. J. Jolly, S. Creigh and A. Mingay, *Age as a Factor in Employment*, Department of Employment, 1980, pp. 22–4.

18. *Employment Patterns*, II, pp. 1–2.

19. *Ageing International*, December 1988, p. 3.

It is difficult, of course, to identify the more covert forms of discrimination emanating from the perception that 'the dynamic contribution' came 'from the people under 35 and that the over-45s are, to some extent, passengers on the superannuation train'.[20] It is clear, however, that by the late 1980s discrimination, both covert and overt, had reached alarming proportions. There was talk of the TOAFFs – those who were 'too old at forty-five'.[21] There was discussion of the relationship between age, recruitment, training and promotion. 'I think the most useful "break" is at the age of 45', explained one expert. 'After that, comes the age at which people are no longer seen as a suitable investment by employers.'[22]

It is more difficult than it seems to account for the growth of ageism since the 1970s. It appears that the explanation once again is more structural than ideological, with employers' attitudes determined chiefly by changes in the nature of the labour market. However, the key no longer lay in the physical demands of work. For if the growth of white-collar employment is used to explain the stability of age discrimination during the first three-quarters of the century, the continuing growth of white-collar employment can scarcely be offered as an explanation for the increase in discrimination that took place from the 1970s onwards. The key lay now, it seems, in the availability – or rather the non-availability – of work that resulted from the depression of the early 1980s. This was a depression that struck particularly hard at industries such as mining and manufacturing which employed a particularly high number of middle-aged workers.[23]

These findings are of considerable significance. If there was no increase in workplace discrimination before 1960 or 1970, it seems likely that during the first sixty or seventy years of the century improvements in the material conditions of the population as a whole benefited the middle aged as much as, if not more than, those from other age groups.

Such a contention receives support from the fact that during the first sixty to seventy years of the century there was no decline in the proportion of the middle aged who were in paid employment. In fact, Figure 4.2 suggests that until 1971 or 1981 there was an

20. *Employment Patterns*, II, p. 29, Nicholas Bosanquet. Also *Ageing International*, December 1988, p. 3; *Weekend*, 3 December 1988.
21. *Weekend*, 3 December 1988.
22. *Employment Patterns*, II, p. 29, Nicholas Bosanquet. Also *Guardian*, 18 March, 30 August, 4 September 1995; *Independent*, 7 August 1995; *Daily Telegraph*, 8 September 1995.
23. See, for example, *Ministry of Labour Gazette*, February 1952.

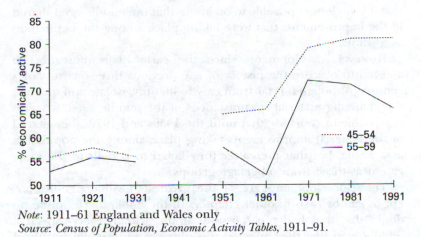

Note: 1911–61 England and Wales only
Source: *Census of Population, Economic Activity Tables*, 1911–91.

Figure 4.2   *Middle-aged economic activity, 1911–91*

increase, rather than a decrease, in the proportion of those in their late forties and fifties who were recorded as economically active.

This finding too is of considerable importance. If there was no increase in workplace discrimination against the middle aged before 1960 or 1970, and an increase in the economic activity rates of the middle aged until 1970 or 1980, it seems very likely that middle-aged workers shared in the more general improvement in material conditions that was enjoyed by the population as a whole during the first seventy to eighty years of the century.

However, this convergence between the material circumstances of the middle aged and the material circumstances of the population as a whole did not survive the depression of the early 1980s. From the 1980s onwards, the material conditions of the late middle aged and the material conditions of the population as a whole began to diverge. As John Burnett has pointed out, 'Unemployment strikes unequally but not randomly. In the modern period age is the principal determinant, the young and the "old" being especially vulnerable.'[24] Figure 4.2 shows that between 1981 and 1991 the proportion of those aged 45–54 recorded as economically active declined just fractionally, while the proportion of those aged 55–59 who were recorded in this way declined by over 7 per cent. These were most crucial developments, for they mean, of course,

24. J. Burnett, *Idle Hands: The Experience of Unemployment, 1790–1990*, Routledge, 1994, p. 272.

that it is no longer possible to maintain that the middle aged shared in the improvements that were taking place among the population as a whole.

However, developments since the early 1980s must not be allowed to obscure the history of the previous three-quarters of a century. Although it is far from easy to identify, isolate and quantify the changing material circumstances of the middle aged, it seems reasonable to conclude that until the 1960s and 1970s they shared in the material improvements taking place among the population as a whole, but that thereafter they failed to benefit to the same extent as those from other age groups.

These developments are of the greatest possible significance. For as can be seen in other chapters of the book, there can be no doubt that they had repercussions upon virtually every aspect of middle-aged life: they affected the physical and mental health of those in their forties and fifties, the nature of their family and other relationships, and their attitudes towards their own, and other people's, circumstances, plans and prospects.

The economic life cycle

There is no doubt either that the standard of living in middle-aged households tended to be higher than in those headed by young adults or the elderly. The middle aged benefited in three distinct, yet complementary ways: the incomes of those in early and late middle age tended to be higher than those of the population as a whole; the expenses of those in late middle age tended to be lower than those of families with children and teenagers who were not working; and this meant that the assets and savings of those in late middle age tended to be worth a good deal more than those to be found in households at other stages of the life cycle.

It can be shown without too much difficulty that the incomes of middle-aged households tended to be higher than those of the population as a whole. Of course, the incomes of middle-aged households, like those of other age groups, varied according to the number, age, ethnicity, gender and class of those belonging to the household. Yet this worked to the advantage of those in their middle years: middle-aged households tended to contain more of the economically active, and fewer of the economically inactive, than those headed by the young and the old. It was middle-aged households that contained teenage children,[25] and as Seebohm Rowntree pointed out at the beginning of the century, it was teenage children who, when working, helped to enhance the standard of living of middle-aged households.

> While the children are earning, and before they leave home to marry, the man [and his wife] enjoys another period of prosperity – possibly, however, only to sink back again into poverty when his children have married and left him . . .[26]

However, it is only from the middle of the century that it is possible to plot the scale of this middle-aged advantage with any degree of precision. It is only from the 1950s that the material circumstances of the middle aged – and other age groups – began to attract the detailed attention of statisticians, market researchers and others interested in the consumer behaviour of the British population. In his pioneering investigation of the relationship between age, income, saving and wealth, Harold Lydall concluded in the early 1950s that, 'As people pass from youth to middle-age, and thence to old age and senility, their economic behaviour passes through various phases. The pattern of these changes is sufficiently stable in any one country and period to warrant our dignifying it with the title of an "economic life cycle".'

> Broadly, the course of events is as follows: Emerging from adolescence, the young adult goes out to work. His first earnings are usually lower than those he will gain later. As he grows in skill and experience he earns more; but at some stage he reaches a peak from which his income begins to fall. This may be due to a decline in his skill or in his strength, or to the onset of periods of illness or unemployment.[27]

As Lydall went on to reveal, the incomes of households headed by those aged 35–44 were 32 per cent higher, and the incomes of households headed by those aged 45–54 were 29 per cent higher, than the incomes of the average British household.[28]

25. A. H. Halsey, *Change in British Society*, Oxford University Press, Oxford, 1986, p. 106.
26. B. S. Rowntree, *Poverty: A Study of Town Life*, Macmillan, London, 1902, p. 136–8. Also G. D. H. Cole and M. I. Cole, *The Condition of Britain*, Gollancz, 1937, p. 253; A. R. Griffin and C. P. Griffin, 'A Social and Economic History of Eastwood and the Nottinghamshire Mining Country', in K. Sagar (ed.), *A D.H. Lawrence Handbook*, Manchester University Press, Manchester, 1982, pp. 134–5.
27. H. Lydall, 'The Life Cycle in Income, Saving, and Asset Ownership', *Economica*, 23, 1955, pp. 132–3.
28. Lydall, 'Life Cycle', p. 141.

Nor was this some peculiarity of the 1950s. When the Institute
for Employment Research at Warwick University examined the
evidence collected by the New Earnings Survey between 1975 and
1990, it concluded that 'The profile of earnings across age-groups
at a given date, with its familiar parabolic shape, has been widely
documented for Britain and many other countries, and for a variety
of time-periods'.[29]

It is unfortunate, of course, that it is possible to offer virtually no
statistical evidence to support the contention that the expenses of
those in late middle age tended to be lower than those of families
with non-working children to look after.[30] However, this is no reason
to doubt the strength of the argument that is being proposed. It is
clear that expenses, like incomes, varied according to the number,
age, gender and class of those belonging to the household. So
although the cost of personal health care and looking after elderly
parents often increased in middle age, the cost of childcare, education, setting up home and repaying mortgage and other loans
almost certainly decreased.[31] As Lydall explained in 1955, 'the number of dependents declines more rapidly than income, expenditure
on durables also falls away, and people begin to put aside larger
sums for their old age'.[32] As one enthusiastic proponent of targeting the over-50 market pointed out thirty years later, 'Because of
no or small mortgage payments, a lifetime accumulation of household furnishings and equipment, and smaller households, many
older persons have more discretionary money to spend than do
younger people'.[33]

Fortunately, it can be shown with some certainty that the possessions and savings – and thus the net assets – of those in middle age
were usually worth a good deal more than those of households at
other stages of the life cycle. Indeed, it is generally recognised that
wealth tended to increase with age, since most people accumulated
property, personal possessions, savings, pension rights and so on
during the course of their working lives. Children usually received
whatever inheritances they were entitled to when in their forties

29. P. Elias and M. Gregory, *The Changing Structure of Occupations and Earnings in
Great Britain, 1975–1990: An Analysis Based on the New Earnings Survey Panel Dataset,*
University of Warwick, Coventry, 1994, p. 36.
30. H. Cunningham, *Children and Childhood in Western Society since 1500,* Longman,
1995, pp. 177–8.
31. See, for example, Mintel, 'Empty Nesters', *Mintel,* 1990.
32. Lydall, 'Life Cycle', p. 150. Also S. F. Buck, 'The Affluent Middle Aged: Spending and Saving Patterns', *ADMAP,* March 1981.
33. M. W. Mauksch, 'The Ageing Population: The New Growth Market', *Ageing
International,* Winter 1987, p. 23.

and fifties, house purchase was normally completed by the age of sixty or sixty-five, and savings tended to peak at the time of retirement, diminishing thereafter as they were drawn upon in order to finance expenditure in old age.[34] Once again, however, it is only from the middle of the century that it is possible to plot the scale of such middle-age advantage with any degree of precision. When Lydall examined the relationship between age, income and saving, he found that, 'While income rises from youth to middle-age and then declines, saving follows an irregular path, probably reaching its summit rather later in life. . . . Its general trend is to increase in middle age, especially in the latter part of this period, and to decline sharply in old age.'[35] He concluded that the net assets of households headed by those aged 45–54 were 45 per cent higher, and the assets of households headed by those aged 55–64 were 55 per cent higher than those of the average household in the sample that he investigated.[36]

When market researchers rediscovered the middle-aged market in the 1980s, they were struck by the fact that 'people in the ten or fifteen years before retirement are not only physically and economically very active; they also have greater discretionary spending power, since their mortgages are paid off and their children grown up'.[37] The trouble, from the marketer researchers' point of view, was that this 'surplus income then goes into savings rather than into consumption'.[38] In 1980, for instance, the building society savings of those aged between 45 and 54 were almost ten per cent higher, and the savings of those aged between 55 and 64 were almost 80 per cent higher, than those of the population as a whole.[39]

Targeting the middle aged

It was this propensity for saving, rather than consumption, that made the middle aged of such interest to producers, suppliers and advertisers. Yet it is an interest that seems easily overlooked by

34. Benson, *Consumer Society*, p. 19; M. Anderson, 'The Emergence of the Modern Life Cycle in Britain', *Social History*, 10, 1985, p. 76.

35. Lydall, 'Life Cycle', pp, 133, 149 Also 'Insurance', *Mintel*, January 1985, p. 70.

36. Lydall, 'Life Cycle', p. 143.

37. H. Lind, 'Media Research and the Affluent Middle Aged', *ADMAP*, February 1981, p. 66. Also Buck, 'Affluent Middle Class'; Office of Population Censuses and Surveys, *The General Household Survey*, HMSO, 1972–95; *The Times*, 6 August 1996.

38. Buck, 'Affluent Middle Class', p. 129.

39. M. Hughes, 'Selling Savings Products to the Older Investor', *ADMAP*, April 1981, See also *Mintel*, June 1982, pp. 66–8; January 1995, p. 69; Key Note Market Report, *The Grey Market in the UK*, Key Note, London, 1994.

commentators on the relationship between age and the economy. Even those interested in the segmentation of the market by age tend either to focus their attention upon adolescents and the elderly,[40] or to deny explicitly that marketing has ever been directed at the middle aged.[41] In fact, the truth is a good deal more complex than either of these approaches suggest, with the middle aged the focus of longstanding, increasing and important commercial interest.

Producers, suppliers and advertisers made specific, and significant efforts to target the middle-aged consumer. It was seen in Chapter 2 that although middle age became associated with decline and decay, many believed that such undesirable characteristics could be mitigated, if not avoided completely, given the adoption of the appropriate remedial action. Those with an eye for the middle-aged market concentrated first upon products designed to improve the appearance of upper and middle-class women, and diversified later into goods and services claiming to protect the physical and financial well-being of all those in their forties and fifties, whether they were male or female, upper-class, middle-class or working-class.

From the earliest years of the century, middle-class, middle-aged women were identified as an important market, with periodicals such as *Queen, The Lady* and *Woman's Own* carrying articles and advertisements promising to conceal the more unattractive features of the middle years. Greying hair could be darkened,[42] the expanding figure could be restrained and disguised: as readers of *Queen* were told in 1910, 'the Sandow corset is the ideal garment for the growing girl, the matron, and the middle-aged or even elderly'.[43] A few years later, *Woman's Own* published a feature on 'pretty styles' for 'the middle-aged woman': 'The high collar, which is gradually regaining favour, is perhaps welcomed more by the woman in years than by her younger sisters.'[44]

By the 1930s, new products had been developed, new markets identified, and new advertising outlets employed. Women from all classes were told how to conceal the grey hair and control the expanding waistline that revealed so glaringly the onset of middle

40. Benson, *Consumer Society*, ch. 2; Cunningham, *Children*, p. 183.
41. G. Greer, *The Change: Women, Ageing and the Menopause*, Penguin, 1992, pp. 345–6.
42. *Woman's Own*, 15 August 1914. Also 18 July 1914; *The Lady*, 2 February 1911. The *Daily Mail* carried the same, or similar, advertisements: see 4 May 1905, 10 April 1908, 5 January 1915.
43. *Queen*, 29 January 1910. Also *Woman's Own*, 10 January 1914.
44. *Woman's Own*, 20 February 1915. Also 3 January, 7 February, 23 May, 3 July, 15 August 1914.

age.[45] Women from all classes were urged to consider health as well as appearance, prevention as well as concealment. The makers of beauty products began to promise that they could eliminate, as well as disguise the tell-tale signs of ageing. 'No longer is beauty considered the prerogative of youth', readers of the *Daily Mail* were assured in 1935.

> Modern woman demands and obtains beauty throughout the years. . . . Signs of age first show themselves in a neglected complexion, but if you give your skin correct care it is utterly unnecessary to submit to the crowsfeet lines and wrinkles that so often scar the mature woman's complexion. At forty you may look twenty . . .[46]

Fifty years later, Empathy Special Care cosmetics were developed with the over-40s particularly in mind: 'these tiny wrinkles and laughter-lines that add character to the face mustn't be allowed to get out of hand'.[47]

The makers of medical and quasi-medical products began to make increasing play of the fact that middle age needed to be taken very seriously indeed. Phyllosan led the way, with Dr Williams' Pink Pills following not far behind. 'NEW LIFE AT 45', they promised in 1935. 'When a woman reaches the critical years of middle age, vague fears often unsettle her. She gets frequent headaches, her back feels fit to break, and she has fits of depression and irritability.'[48] Such devices were widely imitated. Dr Cassell's Tablets claimed to banish 'middle-aged tiredness, ill-health, depression, for good',[49] while de Kuyper's gin promised to bring particular benefits to 'women of middle age' who 'have learnt with reason to rely on de Kuyper's as their best friend in the troubles which come to them at that time'.[50]

It was upon the basis of such promises to conceal, repair and prevent the ravages of middle age that fortunes were made and lost.

45. *Daily Mail*, 3 January 1925; *Sunday Graphic*, 25 January, 8 March, 6 September 1931; *Woman's Journal*, September 1933, July and September 1937; *Woman's Way*, 16 February, 23 and 30 March 1935; *Woman*, 12 and 26 February 1938, 20 April 1940.

46. *Daily Mail*, 29 April 1935. See also *John Bull*, 22 March 1930, 6 April 1940; *Woman*, 13 January, 23 March 1940; 26 April 1947; *Sunday Graphic*, 1 February 1948.

47. *Weekend*, 5 November 1988. Also *Woman*, 25 October 1958, 20 February 1960; *Daily Mail*, 27 June 1950; *Daily Sketch*, 20 February 1970; *Marie Claire*, April 1994.

48. *Woman*, 2 April 1938; *Woman's Way*, 26 January 1935. Also 23 March 1935; *John Bull*, 26 April 1930; *Daily Herald*, 6 June 1942; *Tit-Bits*, 19 January, 16 March 1935; *Sunday Graphic*, 29 September 1935.

49. *Sunday Graphic*, 11 January 1931.

50. *Woman's Journal*, September 1933. Also *Sunday Graphic*, 13 October 1935; *Tit-Bits*, 26 January 1933. Cf. *Daily Mail*, 1 January 1935; *Woman*, 19 March 1938.

As the *Lancet* remarked of hormone replacement therapy in 1975, 'The prospect of universal treatment of a large section of the female population is clearly a glittering commercial prize for the pharmaceutical manufacturer'.[51] It was a prize which was pursued with some relish. Indeed, by 1996 one firm was distributing a series of 'fact sheets' extolling the virtues of hormone replacement therapy which, it was claimed, helped not only with incontinence and osteoporosis but also with hot flushes, mood changes and sexual difficulties.[52]

Men too were targeted. Middle-class men, like middle-class women, have long been offered ways of concealing changes to their hair. As one advertiser pointed out in 1914, 'The whole world today looks askance at the grey-headed, especially the great social and commercial world, where the race for success is becoming daily more strenuous'.[53] Later in the century, working-class men, like working-class women, were assured that they could disguise the unwelcome signs of ageing. 'Baldness is bound to overtake you unless you do something to stop falling hair now', readers of *John Bull* were warned by Silvikrin in 1950.[54] If shampoo did not do the trick, hair could be replaced and bald patches covered up. In 1965, the makers of the Crown Topper reassured potential purchasers that they need have no fear of embarrassment.

> You will be wearing the same style hairpiece as many of the leading stars of TV, the Cinema and the West End. You can sleep in it and even enjoy sports in it! The Crown Topper makes you look and feel at least TEN YEARS younger – even your barber will not know.[55]

Men, like women, were urged to consider other ways of concealing the onset of middle age. At fifty, they were told, they could have 'the energy and looks of 35' with the Vita-Brace abdominal belt: 'it couples the experience of years with the vigorous activeness of youth'.[56] Even the problems of the prostate were not insurmountable.

51. *Lancet*, 7 June 1975.
52. 'Fact Sheets' distributed by Organon Laboratories. Also *Guardian*, 24 February 1996. Cf. information pack from the Herbal Health Clinic, Slough.
53. *Woman's Own*, 18 July 1914. Also *Daily Mail*, 2 January 1905; *Punch*, 16 February 1910.
54. *John Bull*, 27 May 1950. Also *Daily Mail*, 29 June 1950; *Sunday Graphic*, 4 June 1951; *Daily Sketch*, 3 February 1959.
55. *Daily Mail*, 2 September 1965. Also *Sun*, 4, 10 October 1966, 17 March 1975, 4 March 1985; *Daily Sketch*, 25 February 1970.
56. *John Bull*, 6 April 1940. Also 28 June 1930, 28 January 1950; *Picture Post*, 9 December 1939.

IF YOU SUFFER PROSTATE PROBLEMS SUCH AS:

- getting up nights to urinate
- urgency and frequency
- delay and dribbling
- pain and discomfort

you should know about a new book, *Your Prostate: What Every Man Over 40 Needs To Know Now!*[57]

However, the most striking development was the emergence of goods and services which were designed to appeal to most, if not all, of those who were middle-aged. The manufacturers of hair, medical and quasi-medical treatments claimed from the 1930s onwards that their products would benefit all who were in their forties and fifties. Men and women on 'the sunny side of 40' could avoid constipation by taking bile beans or eating Kellogg's All-Bran.[58] Men and women alike would benefit from using indigestion tablets. 'Like a lot of people in the middle years of life, I work too hard. Much too hard', confessed television personality Gilbert Harding in 1960. 'I rush from one stupid place to another and I get indigestion. But I take good care I don't suffer from it. Oh, no, I carry Macleans Tablets around in my pocket.'[59]

Then, during the 1980s and 1990s, middle-aged men and women were identified as prospective consumers, on a significant scale, of a greatly expanded range of leisure goods and financial services.[60] The manufacturing and leisure industries' wooing of the middle aged took several forms. The makers of greeting cards marked out the middle aged as their most important market.[61] The manufacturers of sporting goods and equipment made determined efforts to target those wishing to get fit and fight off middle-age spread.[62] The music industry began to recognise the importance of the 'grey' market: record companies brought out re-releases, and disc

57. *Observer,* 27 February 1994. Also A. Montague, 'When Life's No Ups and All Downs', *Guardian,* 9 July 1996.

58. *Sunday Graphic,* 14 July 1935, 19 January 1958, 9 January 1960; *Daily Sketch,* 10 February 1959.

59. *Daily Mail,* 6 January 1960.

60. Lind, 'Media Research'; W. Gordon, 'The Life-style of the Affluent Middle Aged', *ADMAP,* February 1981; Mauksch, 'Ageing Population'; C. D'Souza, 'Age Cannot Wither Them', *Sunday Times, Style,* 27 August 1995; 'Old Rockers in the Spotlight', *Observer,* 10 September 1995; D. Coyle, 'Baby Boomers on a Spending Spree', *Independent,* 10 January 1996.

61. Information from Roger Seddon, United Greeting Card Co., Berkhamsted, November 1995.

62. *Athletics Weekly,* 20 April 1985.

jockeys played 'golden oldies' designed to appeal to those anxious
to recapture something of their youth.[63] By the 1990s, there was 'a
huge market for old-name bands to play corporate hospitality piss-
ups, holiday camps, even bingo halls to audiences who have no
desire to get sweaty over today's musicians'.[64] Other entrepreneurs
too were determined to exploit the opportunities opening up before
them. The owners of restaurants like the Beefeater chain saw new
ways of courting the late middle aged.

> When there's more time to relax, enjoy your leisure time, make new
> friends and appreciate life to the full . . . the Beefeater Emerald Club
> could be for you.
>   By joining the Beefeater Emerald Club, you will be able to enjoy
> quality food and wine with exclusive members offers.[65]

The travel industry's wooing of the so-called 'mature market' is
more firmly established. Saga has long been the market leader in
travel for the elderly, and during the 1990s the company began to
turn its attention to the late middle aged.

> Founded more than 40 years ago, today Saga is an international
> organisation with offices in Britain and the USA providing a range
> of services for people aged 50 and over . . .
>   Saga holidays are offered at the time of your life when you can seek
> out new and exciting travel opportunities, enjoy the company of old
> and new friends and have the freedom to broaden your horizons.[66]

However, the most striking feature of the revival of interest
in the mature market has been the attempt by those involved in
financial services to target the middle-aged, and especially the late
middle-aged, consumer. The insurance industry led the way. Home
insurers, for instance, made great efforts to attract clients among
the over-fifties. As one underwriter explained, 'Older people are not
only more honest but they don't claim for every little thing. They
use their insurance for catastrophes but not for maintenance.'[67] One
new scheme, 'Advantage 55', was developed, it was claimed, because
'we know people aged 55 or over take better care of their homes'.
Those interested in receiving a quotation had only to phone a free
– and, it was hoped, easily remembered – number: 0500 55 55 00.[68]

63. *Sun*, 1 March 1975, 1 March 1985.
64. *Independent on Sunday*, 10 December 1995. Also *Sunday Times*, 3 March 1996.
65. Beefeater publicity leaflet, 1996.   66. *A World of Holidays from Saga*, 1995.
67. H. Thompson, 'Home Insurers Woo Over-50s', *Sunday Times*, 13 November
1994.
68. Leaflet by Landmark Express, 1994. Also *The Times*, 1 November 1994. For
Saga's involvement, see *Daily Express*, 27 June 1995; *The Times*, 3 June, 21 August 1995.

Life insurers, medical insurers and motor insurers also saw the possibilities before them in the 1990s. Sun Life advertised its 'Guaranteed Over 50 Plan' under the headline, 'Congratulations! You've reached the age when your acceptance for low cost life cover is GUARANTEED without a medical!'[69] Landmark Express announced that it was offering a 'Reward for experienced drivers over 45. Exceptional Motor insurance. Pay Less, Get More.'[70]

It is a simple fact. If you are over 45, you are subsidising the mistakes of less-experienced drivers. And you will almost certainly be paying a much higher motor insurance premium as a result of this – unless, of course, you arrange your cover with Landmark Express.[71]

Direct Line Insurance promoted its '70% discount for mature drivers' with rhetoric that was almost exactly the same.

If you are over 50, the chances are you will have had a lot more driving experience than the average motorist. That's why we have increased the level of our maximum no claim discount from 65% to 70% for mature drivers, the only major insurer to do so.[72]

Other organisations and individuals dealt implicitly, rather than explicitly, with the middle-aged market. So while it is true that producers, suppliers and advertisers often thought of their customers less as middle-aged than as men or women, town-dwellers or country-dwellers, middle-class or working-class and so on, they were in fact often catering for the middle aged. When farmers grew their food, railway companies ran their trains, motor manufacturers made their cars, grocers opened their shops and tour operators organised their holidays, they did so, at least in part, with the middle-aged consumer very much in mind. Even though manufacturers, suppliers and advertisers did not always identify their middle-aged consumers as middle-aged, they knew that the 'mature' market was of considerable, albeit easily overlooked, significance. It is a significance whose scale, once again, can be gauged only during the second half of the century.

It was not just that the middle aged spent more than the average consumer upon products such as alcohol, do-it-yourself, books and newspapers, and eating out.[73] They also tended to spend more than the average upon products such as motor cars and long-distance

69. Leaflet by Sun Life, 1994. Also *Sun*, 6 March 1985; S. Colbeck, 'Premium Customers', *The Times*, 27 May 1995.

70. *Sun*, 15 November 1994. Also *Guardian*, 7 November 1994.

71. Leaflet by Landmark Express, 1995.　　72. *Daily Mirror*, 11 August 1994.

73. Office of Population Censuses and Surveys, *Household Survey*, 1972–95; Mintel, *Empty Nesters; The Times*, 6 August 1996.

travel. By the 1970s, it was middle-aged men who bought many of the cars that were sold: surveys carried out in 1974 and 1978 reported that men aged 45–54 were up to a quarter more likely than men generally to own their own car.[74] Indeed, a Mori poll conducted during the early 1990s revealed that 'the over-fifties are almost twice as likely to buy a new car as younger drivers: 38% of over-fifties buy a new car, compared with only 20 per cent of the under-fifties'.[75] By the 1990s, it was the middle aged and elderly who accounted for much of the growth in long-haul flying. 'Rucksack, sarong, round-the-world ticket, guide book, student card . . . hold it right there.'

> Independent travel, once the preserve of adventurous youth, is becoming a hit with a more mature generation. Forty per cent of long-haul flights are now sold to over-45s and, according to Roger Heape, managing director of British Airways Holidays, 'the fogey, or grey, market is now leading the way in terms of more adventurous holiday experiences'.[76]

It is by using evidence such as this that it is possible to begin to disentangle the relationship between middle age, work, wealth and consumption. In fact, it seems that certain broad generalisations may now be made with a considerable degree of confidence. The middle aged tended to share in the more general improvement in material conditions that took place during the course of the twentieth century, they tended to be better off than their contemporaries at other stages of the life cycle, and they tended to attract much more commercial interest than has usually been recognised.

Women's double disadvantage

However, the relationship between middle age, work, wealth and consumption was a good deal more complicated than such generalisations suggest. For despite the improvement and advantage discussed above, middle age was a period during which gender and class differences tended to become still more pronounced than when people were younger. Unfortunately, the difference between male and female standards of living is one of those aspects of middle age which it is difficult to discuss without so much qualification that it

---

74. 'Cars', *Mintel*, May 1978.
75. J. Clarkson, 'No Roadster Like an Old Roadster', *Sunday Times*, 11 September 1994.
76. *Observer*, 30 July 1995.

begins to look suspiciously like obfuscation.[77] On the one hand, it can be shown that the material circumstances of men and women both improved and converged during the course of the century.[78] On the other hand, it needs to be stressed that women were nearly always worse off than men, and that the gap between male and female standards of living tended to become wider in middle age than at earlier stages of the life cycle.

It is no surprise, of course, to learn that middle-aged women were discriminated against on account of their gender, and that this meant that they tended to be worse off than men of their own age. It is no surprise either to learn that middle-aged women were discriminated against on account of their age, and that this meant that they tended to be worse off than women who had yet to enter middle age. However, what may come as something of a surprise is the scale and significance of this double disadvantage, for it meant that middle age was a period during which the material circum-stances of men and women tended, not to converge, but to diverge, and diverge significantly.[79]

This growing gap between male and female standards of living manifested itself in a number of ways. As they grew older, married women tended to earn less, possess less, and exercise less economic power than men of the same age. The situation was even worse for single, widowed and divorced women: as they grew older, they tended not only to earn less and possess less than men of the same age but also to have to budget alone for all the expenses that they and their families incurred.

Indeed, whether they were married or single, widowed or divorced (middle-class or working-class), women in their middle years faced particular difficulties in obtaining and retaining well-paid employ-ment. They face discrimination, both informal and formal, subtle and unsubtle, that made it more difficult for them than for younger women or for men of their own age.

It should not be forgotten, however, that women benefited as well as suffered from the popular stereotyping of the middle aged. They benefited in so far as middle age was associated, to some degree at least, with steadiness, reliability and respectability, an association which resulted in some employers specifying that only

77. L. Stamm and C. D. Ryff, 'Introduction: An Interdisciplinary Perspective on Women's Power and Influence', in L. Stamm and C. D. Ryff (eds), *Social Power and Influence of Women*, Westview Press, Boulder, CO, 1984.

78. Benson, *Consumer Society*, ch. 1.

79. M. Bernard, C. Itzin, C. Phillipson and J. Skucha, 'Gendered Work, Gendered Retirement', in S. Arber and J. Ginn (eds), *Connecting Gender and Ageing: A Sociological Approach*, Oxford University Press, Oxford, 1995, p. 59.

middle-aged women should apply for jobs in domestic service.[80] It was an association which resulted too in public sector employers like the prison service being prepared to recruit women, though not men, into their late forties, and in a few late twentieth-century banks and retailers instituting policies to recruit older women (and men) 'on the grounds that they are more dependable and politer to the customers'.[81]

Middle-aged women also benefited in so far as it is possible to regard casual and part-time employment as desirable or as preferable to no employment at all. In fact, one of the most striking features of the twentieth-century labour market has been the transformation which has taken place in the gender composition of the workforce. Figure 4.3 shows that while the economic activity rates of middle-aged men changed scarcely at all during the first eighty years of the century, the rates of 45–54-year-old women increased almost exactly four times. Whereas in 1911 only 18 per cent of 45–54-year-old women were recorded as economically active, by 1951 the figure had risen to 28 per cent, and by 1991 to 71 per cent. It was a remarkable transformation, a transformation which, whether it was welcomed or resented, and whether it involved part-time or full-time work, did a good deal to improve, or at least to maintain, the living standards of middle-aged women.

Most often, of course, women suffered, and suffered severely, from popular attitudes towards the middle aged. It was seen in Chapter 2 that although the middle aged of both sexes were held to fall prey to a broadly similar set of physical and psychological failings, middle-aged women were believed to suffer too from a number of specific physical and emotional difficulties, most of which stemmed in one way or another from the menopause. Employers were no more immune than anybody else to the influence of such negative stereotyping. Although the scale and significance of discrimination varied from industry to industry, employer to employer and period to period, women discovered time and time again that when they reached their forties – or even their thirties – they were likely to face particular difficulties in obtaining, and retaining, the jobs that they wanted.[82]

80. For example, *The Times*, 6 May 1915; *Mail on Sunday*, 6 October 1996.
81. *Sun*, 3 October 1966, 4 March 1975; *Daily Sketch*, 23 February 1979; C. Eagar, 'Rebirth of the Baby Boomers', *Observer*, 17 July 1994.
82. Investigations by the National Advisory Committee on the Employment of Older Men and Women in 1953 and the Employment Committee of the House of Commons in 1989 stressed too the importance of inflexible pension arrangements and wage scales based on age, rather than length of service. Also Bernard *et al.*, 'Gendered Work', pp. 61–3.

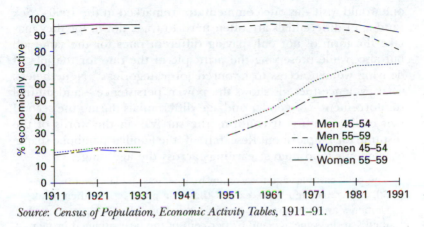

Source: *Census of Population, Economic Activity Tables*, 1911–91.

Figure 4.3   *Middle-aged men's and women's economic activity, 1911–91*

It is possible to point to a continuous, albeit intermittent, public commentary on the discrimination faced by middle-aged women. In 1930, *John Bull* ran a special report on 'The Women with the Nightmare Birthday' – forty of course. It concluded that 'women workers in every trade or occupation have bitter cause to dread the approach of age', and it castigated 'The girl who, with a mouthful of false teeth, sneers at the tinted hair of her colleague would feel small and cheap if she had the imagination to see into the secret thoughts of the older women'.[83] In the 1950s, the National Advisory Committee on the Employment of Older Men and Women discussed in considerable detail the age barriers that women faced.[84] It was common throughout industry, reported the *British Medical Journal*, to decline to employ women over thirty-five because of their menopausal irritability.[85]

Nor was this all. Whether they worked full-time or part-time, women in their forties and fifties were unlikely to be as well paid as younger women or as men of their own age, Indeed, the gap between men's and women's earnings tended to grow wider in middle age. It is a pity that the evidence available to support this claim is less comprehensive and more elusive and ambiguous than

83. *John Bull*, 14 June 1930.

84. *National Advisory Committee, First Report*, 1953, p. 19. Also *Ministry of Labour Gazette*, February 1952.

85. Joan Malleson in *British Medical Journal*, 15 December 1956. Also *National Advisory Committee, First Report*, 1953, p. 18; *Lancet*, 24 October 1953. Age-based salary scales and pension schemes also worked to the disadvantage of the middle aged.

one would wish – as one commentator remarked in the 1960s, 'Sex
[and age] differentials are often hard to track down, for they may
take the form of not only paying different rates for the same job
but also, while preserving the principle of the rate for the job, of
denying women access to favoured job categories'.[86] Nonetheless,
what evidence there is shows the power, persistence – and mutual
reinforcement – of gender and age differentials during the second
half of the century. It confirms the survival, in the words of the
Institute for Employment Research, of 'the familiar parabolic shape'
of women's (and men's) earnings across the age range.

> The peak earnings age for women in 1990 was the late twenties, 28–
> 30, more than ten years earlier than for men. . . . At their peak,
> women's average earnings of £5.65 per hour were 82 per cent of
> men's at the same age and 67 per cent of the peak attained by men
> more than ten years older.[87]

This combination of ageism and sexism had a profound effect
upon the earnings of middle-aged women. Married women had to
contend not only with the ageism and sexism directed at all middle-
aged women, but also with the ageism and sexism directed specifically at those who were married. The marriage bar – the ban on the
employment of married women – remained remarkably resilient.
Usually, of course, this particular form of discrimination had its
impact well before the onset of middle age – most women, after all,
married while in their early-mid twenties.[88] However, this does not
mean that middle-aged women avoided its deleterious consequences.
They continued to be at a disadvantage if they had been dismissed
or refused work ten, twenty or thirty years before, and had been
unable to find the same, or similar work in the years that followed.
They were discriminated against afresh if they remarried following
divorce or widowhood – and most women who remarried in such
circumstances did so when they were in their forties and early fifties.[89]
    It is easy to underestimate the scale and impact of such discrim-
ination in the years before the Second World War. Elizabeth Roberts
points out that 'The ban in teaching is well known, but less well

86. M. P. Fogarty, 'Portrait of a Pay Structure', in J. L. Meij (ed.), *Internal Wage Structure*, North Holland Publishing Company, Amsterdam, 1963, p. 62.
87. P. Elias and M. Gregory, *The Changing Structure of Occupations and Earnings in Great Britain, 1975–1990: An Analysis Based on the New Earnings Survey Panel Dataset*, Employment Department, 1994, p. 36.
88. R. Schoen and J. Baj, 'Twentieth-Century Cohort Marriage and Divorce in England and Wales', *Population Studies*, 38, 1984, p. 442.
89. Schoen and Baj, 'Marriage and Divorce', p. 442.

known are the policies of *individual* employers who refused, for example, to employ married shop assistants and typists'.[90] Less well known too are the policies operating in the civil service and in municipal employment.[91] In fact, it was not until 1944 that the marriage bar was lifted in teaching, and 1946 that it was abandoned in the civil service.[92]

Married women faced other barriers besides. They had to contend not only with the – more or less overt – discrimination of their employers, but also with the – more or less covert – discrimination of their husbands. It was not just that many husbands, of all ages, exercised considerable control over their wives' spending; it was that as they grew older, many husbands began to take a still closer interest in what their wives were doing. This is less surprising that it may seem for it is a paradox of consumer behaviour that women tended to retain control over household expenditure so long as it remained arduous and challenging, but began to share control with their husbands (and children) when real incomes rose and shopping and other forms of expenditure became less burdensome.[93] It was a paradox that worked to the particular disadvantage of middle-aged women. It was in middle age that household incomes tended to rise, in middle age that basic expenses tended to fall, and in middle age therefore that shopping and other forms of consumption were likely to prove less burdensome and more enjoyable.

Married women were not alone in facing new difficulties in middle age. So too did the growing number of women who found themselves widowed or divorced. However, their problems tended to be rather different: they had to contend less with ageism and sexism directed at their marital status than with the underlying economic and social circumstances in which they found themselves.

The single, widowed and divorced comprised a substantial proportion of the middle-aged female population. It was in middle age after all that significant numbers of women were widowed, and in

90. E. Roberts, *Women's Work 1840–1940*, Macmillan, Basingstoke, 1988, p. 73. Also J. Lewis, *Women in Britain since 1945: Women, Family, Work and the State in the Post-war Years*, Blackwell, Oxford, 1992, p. 68.

91. Ellen Wilkinson in *Sunday Graphic*, 28 June 1931. Also 14 July 1935; *John Bull*, 8 February 1930.

92. Cited K. Orr, 'Working-class Women and Work: Edinburgh, 1911–39', Paper read at Economic History Society Conference, Nottingham University, 1994, p. 8; E. Roberts, *Women and Families: An Oral History, 1940–1970*, Blackwell, Oxford, 1995, pp. 117, 132.

93. Benson, *Consumer Society*, ch. 8.

middle age that the majority of women were divorced.[94] Indeed, throughout the first half of the century a quarter and more of all 45–54-year-old women were either single or widowed.[95] It was in middle age therefore that a substantial minority of women had to cope – or cope again – with being the family breadwinner. Occasionally, widows and divorcees found that they were better off than when they were married.[96] Nearly always of course they, like single women, discovered that their incomes were lower than those of conventional households: women earned less than men, and single women less than married couples, They discovered, however, that their expenses were not necessarily that much lower than those of conventional households: they still had to find somewhere to live, still had to pay their bills, and still very often had to look after their children.

The result was that those who were divorced, widowed or single were a great deal more likely than those who were married to live below, or close to the poverty line. Seebohm Rowntree found, for example, that in turn-of-the-century York, 45 per cent of 'the poorest people in the city' were widows.

> Few people spend all their days in [this] class. . . . It is nevertheless a class into which the poor are at any time liable to sink should misfortune overtake them, such as continued lack of work, or the death or illness of the chief wage-earner.[97]

This relationship between middle age, single parenthood and poverty was weakened, but not removed, by the introduction of state pensions for widows and orphans and other legislation designed to assist the growing number of women who chose, or were forced, to live alone. As *John Bull* explained in 1930, the employers' 'systematic crowding-out of the middle-aged falls particularly hard upon the women who is alone in the world and entirely dependent upon her own earnings'.[98] As A. H. Halsey pointed out in 1986, 'There are now three-quarters of a million one-parent families with dependent children. The woman left to raise children alone is among the most pathetic casualties of an affluent society.'[99]

94. The average age of divorce fell from 47 in the middle of the century to 37 in 1975. Schoen and Baj, 'Marriage and Divorce', p. 442.

95. B. R. Mitchell and P. Deane, *Abstract of British Historical Statistics*, III, 1912, Q. 13,390, C. Chapman.

96. For example, *Royal Commission on Divorce*, Cambridge University Press, Cambridge, 1962, p. 16.

97. Rowntree, *Poverty*, pp. 45, 47.   98. *John Bull*, 14 June 1930.

99. Halsey, *Change*, p. 110. Also Lewis, *Women*, p. 103; L. A. Morgan, *After Marriage Ends: Economic Consequences for Midlife Women*, Sage, 1991.

Working-class retrenchment and middle-class anxiety

The relationship between middle age, work, wealth and consumption is complicated still further by the fact that middle age was a period during which class differences, like gender differences, tended to become more pronounced than they were at earlier stages of the life cycle. Fortunately, however, the gap between middle-class and working-class standards of living is somewhat easier to examine than that between men and women, and so can be discussed without too much qualification or obfuscation.

It has been seen already that the middle aged enjoyed a standard of living that tended both to improve and to be higher than that found in households headed by young adults or the elderly. However, it must be stressed, and stressed most strongly, that once again such improvement and advantage did not work to the benefit of all those in their forties and fifties. The gap between middle-class and working-class standards of living grew wider in middle age: in middle-class households, incomes tended to increase and expenses to decline; in working-class households, incomes tended to decline and expenses to stabilise or decline only slightly.

It is not difficult to show that the gap between middle-class and working-class incomes grew wider in middle age. Although the relationship between age, class and employment changed significantly during the course of the century, it operated consistently, it seems, to the detriment of those from the working class. So although the middle aged of all classes were held to fall prey to a broadly similar set of physical and psychological failings, this worked to the particular disadvantage of the working class. After all, it was working-class work, not middle-class work, that depended, to a greater or lesser degree, upon such 'youthful' qualities as strength, mobility, flexibility and endurance.[100]

Employers were often reluctant to retain, let alone recruit, working-class employees once they reached their forties and fifties. Indeed, such discrimination had a longer history than might be imagined: as early as the middle of the nineteenth century workers were complaining about the class basis of employers' attitudes towards the middle aged.

100. C. L. Cooper and D. P. Torrington (eds), *After Forty: The Time for Achievement*, Wiley, Chichester, 1981, p. 4.

When employers and clerks in their office are compelled to wear
spectacles, it is considered with them an honourable badge; but to
the poor workman it is a sudden death – he is no longer employed.[101]

In fact, employers' attitudes towards failing sight – greying hair and
balding heads – reveal a good deal about the relationship between
age, class and discrimination. The middle class sometimes benefited
from their association with these symbols of ageing.[102] The working
class almost never did. A women who attempted to become the family breadwinner when her husband was made unemployed in the
late 1920s was told that at thirty-one she was 'too old' to work in a
factory.[103] John Burnett points out that throughout the inter-war
years, 'age operated as a limiting employment factor throughout
the span of a man's life'.

> If some were too old at eighteen to twenty-one for work which could
> be done by boys of sixteen to eighteen, men over forty-five faced
> special difficulty in keeping or obtaining jobs where physical strength
> was regarded as more important than skill and experience: in min-
> ing, steelmaking, dock-work and labouring generally older men were
> at a serious disadvantage, despite often pathetic attempts to disguise
> their age by darkening their hair, abandoning the use of spectacles
> and so on.[104]

It was clear by the late 1930s that such discrimination could undermine the basis upon which the economic life cycle of working-class
families was predicated.

> 'Too old at forty' means, in working-class terms, too old at the age
> when the family responsibilities may be beginning at last to diminish.
> It denies the workman that compensation for the struggle of earlier
> years which he used, in middle age, often to enjoy.[105]

Indeed, it has been suggested that in the years following the Second World War, age became the major determinant of unemployment, with young workers and men in late middle age especially

---

101. Cited in *Morning Chronicle*, 18 July 1850. Also *R. C. Labour*, Digest of Evidence,
Group A, III, QQ. 23,303–4, G. Clarke; *R. C. Aged Poor*, III, QQ. 16,576, 16,622,
H. Allen.

102. *Family Doctor*, 25 January 1890. Also 'SENEX' to *Lancet*, 31 August 1901.

103. Burnett, *Idle Hands*, p. 218. Also Orr, 'Women'.

104. Burnett, *Idle Hands*, pp. 217–18. Also C. Forman, *Industrial Town: Self-portrait
of St Helens in the 1920s*, Granada, 1979, p. 67; S. Constantine, *Unemployment in Britain
Between the Wars*, Longman, 1980, p. 24.

105. Cole and Cole, *Condition of Britain*, p. 253.

at risk.[106] The National Advisory Committee on the Employment of Older Men and Women reported in 1953 that,

> The evidence is that in later middle age people tend to move away from occupations which make severe demands for speed, agility or sustained muscular effort, especially where two or all of these requirements are present together.[107]

In fact, there seems little doubt that the association between age and unemployment – or rather between late middle age and working-class unemployment – intensified during the course of the 1970s and 1980s.

> Once unemployed, the older worker has greater difficulty in finding re-employment and many therefore join the ranks of the long-term unemployed. At around fifty it has been argued that the unemployed man enters an 'age trap' – too old for employment, but too young for state benefits until sixty-five.[108]

A fifty-year-old woman put it more succinctly: 'When you're over 50 they don't wish to know – it's either 30, 35 is all right. . . . Over 40 they don't seem to want to know.'[109]

This relationship between age, class and discrimination remains fundamental to any understanding of the material conditions of the middle aged. For despite the publicity given so often to the plight of unemployed managers, professionals and white-collar workers,[110] it was the working class, not the middle class, that suffered disproportionately from the material, physical and psychological deprivations that were brought about by unemployment.

However, it was the desperation of the middle class – not the working class – that most often touched the hearts of contemporary commentators. When *John Bull* discussed discrimination against middle-aged women in 1930, it conceded perfunctorily that 'Even the charwoman over forty often hears the more or less polite negative to her enquiry for work'. It reserved its rhetoric for the plight of clerical workers: the life of Miss K, it explained, was

> one long, anxious struggle against the signs of age, . . . A large portion of her earnings as a shorthand-typist is spent each month on

106. Burnett, *Idle Hands*, p. 272.　107. *National Advisory Committee*, 1953, p.13.
108. Burnett, *Idle Hands*, p. 273. Also 'Modern Times' documentary on Househusbands, BBC2, May 1996.
109. Burnett, *Idle Hands*, p. 274.
110. *Weekend*, 3 December 1988; J. Margolis, 'Middle Class and on the Scrap Heap', *Sunday Times*, 11 September 1994; P. Fisher, 'The Grey and the Good', *Guardian*, 18 March 1995; *Daily Mail*, 4 May 1996.

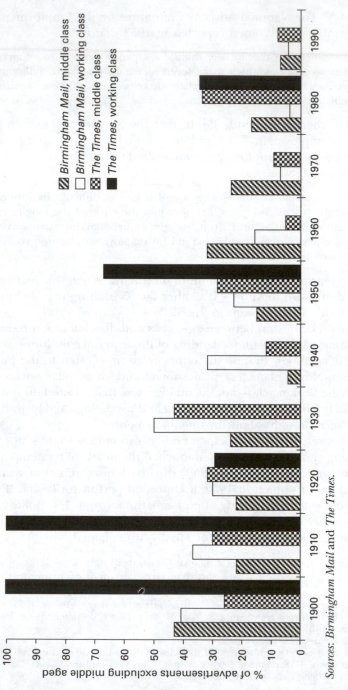

Sources: *Birmingham Mail* and *The Times*.

Figure 4.4   *Job advertisements excluding the middle aged, by class, 1900–90*

keeping the grim, grey shadow in the background. She is forty, but dare not, for one moment, relax her care.[111]

When the *Sunday Graphic* discussed ageism a few years later, it concentrated upon its impact in the City of London. 'The fetish of "youth in business" has assumed such importance in London that the "young" men have taken to the dye-pot to combat the first grey hairs in their eyebrows and moustaches.'[112] Sympathy continued to be dispensed on a class basis. 'This year, many of my friends are reaching 50', reported Graham Sargeant in 1994.

> One or two, riding high in affluence and achievement, are holding good parties. But their guests reveal a different story. For many more, the half century is bringing an end to careers they thought would go on a lot longer and, they hoped, further. To their amazement, they are cast as the fat being shed in the latest corporate diet plan.[113]

The middle class was learning what the middle class had always known, that it was difficult to secure anything approaching a job for life. The *Daily Mail* reflected gloomily in 1996 that, 'A generation ago, men in their 40s were secure. If they were trained and on a career path, they could expect more leisure time and an easier life as they got older.'

> At 45, these men used to think: 'How do I prepare myself for the next promotion?' Now they have to think: 'How do I prepare myself to make a fresh start if I'm made redundant?'[114]

The changing class basis of age discrimination can be illustrated by a reworking and refinement of the analysis of job advertisements that was presented earlier in the chapter. Despite the limitations of the evidence which it presents, Figure 4.4 confirms the broad validity of the arguments that are being put forward. It suggests that during the first half of the century the working class faced greater discrimination than the middle class, but that from the 1950s onwards the balance changed, and may even have been reversed.[115]

The other reason that the gap between middle-class and working-class incomes grew wider in middle age was, of course, that those

111. *John Bull*, 14 June 1930.   112. *Sunday Graphic*, 7 July 1935.

113. *The Times*, 26 September 1994. Also Margolis, 'Middle Class'; W. Hutton, 'Bad Times for the Good Life', *Guardian*, 2 August 1994; *The Times Educational Supplement*, 3 February 1995; Guardian, 30 August 1995; *Independent*, 7 August 1995; R. Powell to *News of the World*, 16 September 1995.

114. *Daily Mail*, 4 May 1996. Also Wolverhampton Oral History Project Mr K.

115. Jolly, et al., *Age*, p. 24.

in middle-class and working-class jobs attained their maximum earnings at very different stages of the life cycle. The more middle-class the job, the later the age at which earnings peaked. There is a good deal of scattered evidence demonstrating the contrasting earnings profiles of middle-class and working-class employees.[116] However, as so often, the only detailed, systematic investigations were carried out during the second half of the century. Fogarty, suggests, for example, that in the early 1950s, white-collar workers attained their peak earnings about the age of fifty, skilled and semi-skilled workers about the age of forty, and unskilled workers about the age of thirty.[117]

It is a great deal more difficult to show that the gap between middle-class and working-class expenses grew wider in middle age. However, the task is by no means impossible. It was seen earlier in the chapter that as they grew older, families might well spend more on personal health care and looking after elderly parents but that they almost certainly spent less on items such as house purchase, child care and their children's education. It follows therefore that because it was the middle class that was most likely to buy their own homes, employ nannies and pay for private education, it was the middle class that would benefit most from the reduction in such spending that occurred in late middle age.[118]

There seems no doubt then that the gap between middle-class and working-class standards of living was wider in middle age than at earlier stages of the life cycle. While the income at the disposal of the middle class tended to rise during middle age, the income at the disposal of the working class tended to stagnate or even to decline. In fact, it seems likely that it was this longstanding – and seemingly pre-ordained – gap between middle-class and working-class standards of living that helps to account for the surprise and alarm with which middle-class unemployment was greeted in the 1980s and 1990s. It seems certain that it was this gap between middle-class and working-class standards of living that makes it possible to reconcile such surprise and alarm with the enthusiasm and ingenuity with which, at exactly the same time, commercial interests began to court so assiduously more and more sections of the middle-aged market.

It is clear therefore that the demographic, health and material developments which have been considered so far tended nearly

116. For example, *Family Doctor*, 19 February 1910; *R. C. Aged Poor*, 1895, Q. 17,559, F. Crompton; information from Paul Johnson.
117. Fogarty, 'Pay Structure', pp. 54, 56. Also *Employment Patterns*, II, p. 90.
118. *R. C. Divorce*, II, 1912, Q. 13,828, W. C. Williams.

always to be mutually reinforcing. It was the growing numbers of the middle aged, their improving health and their increasing prosperity which made the better off middle aged of such interest to the suppliers of an extensive and expanding range of consumer goods and services. It was this interrelationship between demography, health and material circumstances which, it will be seen, helped to determine both the nature of middle-aged relationships and the values and attitudes adopted by those in their forties and fifties.

CHAPTER FIVE

Family Relationships

It seems to be accepted almost without question that middle age brought with it a series of crises in personal relationships. Worried about their looks, frustrated at their physical failings, concerned about their work and dissatisfied with their achievements, the middle aged were said to turn against those closest to them: they become bored with their partners, jealous of their children and neglectful of their parents.[1] Middle age, they were warned, is a time of anxiety, adultery and abrogation, a period of hypochondria, compulsion and dysfunction.[2]

Moreover, it is a commonplace that such crises have become both more common and more serious during the course of the century.[3] Generation upon generation of commentators claimed to identify the weakening of family ties in the face of growing prosperity, rising expectations, the burgeoning youth culture of the young and the increasing longevity of the elderly.[4] In fact, it was claimed so often that divorce rates were rising, juvenile delinqency increasing and neglect of the elderly intensifying that such beliefs have come

---

1. A. Storr, 'A New Life in Middle Age', in R. Owen (ed.), *Middle Age*, BBC, 1967, p. 40; E. Jacques, 'The Mid-life Crisis', in Owen (ed.), *Middle Age*, pp. 33–4; A. S. Rossi, 'Life-span Theories and Women's Lives', *Signs: Journal of Women in Culture and Society*, 6, 1989, p. 11.

2. *Lancet*, 23 October 1943; Consumers' Association, *Living Through Middle Age*, Consumers' Association, 1976, p. 103; Jacques, 'Mid-life Crisis', pp. 33–4.

3. Cf. T. R. Cole, *The Journey of Life: A Cultural History of Aging in America*, Cambridge University Press, Cambridge, 1992, p. 4.

4. Storr, 'New Life', pp. 37–8; J. Obelkevich, 'Consumption', in J. Obelkevich and P. Catterall (eds), *Understanding Post-war British Society*, Routledge, 1994, p. 67; G. Pearson, *Hooligan: A History of Respectable Fears*, Macmillan, Basingstoke, 1983, pp. 34, 55, 219.

to form an integral part of popular views about twentieth-century decay and deterioration.[5]

These of course are most difficult issues with which to deal. The problems they raise are both methodological and empirical. On the one hand, it is not easy to know how best to measure the quality of family relationships, it is difficult to isolate the experiences of the middle aged from those of other age groups, and it is more complicated still to compare such experiences at different stages of the century. On the other hand, family relationships always tended to be private and elusive, the middle aged never attracting as much attention as adolescents or the elderly, and family stability rarely proving anything like as newsworthy as family dislocation.[6]

However, all is not lost. It is helpful to approach the study of middle-aged (and other) relationships by distinguishing clearly between their legal, material and emotional components.[7] It is possible to compensate, to some extent at least, for the empirical difficulties of studying middle-aged relationships by following Arthur Marwick's celebrated injunction to explore the 'unwitting testimony' of the past.[8] The fact that the middle aged never attracted as much attention as adolescents or the elderly can be turned back on itself. Oral studies of teenage life can be used to reveal what young people thought about their middle-aged parents, and social survey investigations into the conditions of the elderly can be used to discover what their middle-aged children were – or were not – doing by way of helping them.

It is believed therefore that it should be possible to comment with some confidence about the family relationships of the middle aged. It will be suggested that popular views of middle age as a time of crisis and maladjustment are seriously misleading. While it will be conceded that the years between forty and sixty brought with them problems in personal relationships, it will be shown how inaccurate it is to depict middle age in terms of dysfunction and dislocation and how difficult it is to establish whether or not such problems increased during the course of the century. Middle age, it will be argued, was as heterogeneous as any other: it was characterised as

---

5. A. P. Thompson, 'Problems of Ageing and Chronic Sickness', *British Medical Journal*, 30 July 1949; *British Medical Journal*, 31 July 1954, 27 May 1961.

6. Thompson, 'Problems'.

7. Cf. D. Jerome, 'Intimate Relationships', in J. Bond and P. Coleman (eds), *Ageing in Society: An Introduction to Social Gerontology*, Sage, 1990.

8. A. Marwick, *The Nature of History*, Macmillan, Basingstoke, 1970, p. 136.

much by secure, stable relationships as those which displayed the classic, and easily recognisable, symptoms of middle-aged *angst*.

There is no denying though that popular views about middle-aged relationships had a certain basis in reality. As everybody knew, it was by no means uncommon for those in their forties and fifties to display some at least of the classic signs of middle-aged dissatisfaction: they became bored with their partners, jealous of their children and neglectful of their parents.

Adultery, separation and divorce

Middle age was a traumatic time in many marriages, with husbands and wives separating, divorcing, launching into affairs and becoming increasingly embittered with one another. Certainly, the press was happy to revel in the marital difficulties of the middle aged. It reported first on individual cases: in 1925, for example, the *Daily Mail* carried a story about a middle-aged woman who was suing her machinist husband for desertion, while he in turn accused her of misconduct with their lodger, a grenadier guardsman. The husband claimed to have found a pair of his wife's shoes under the lodger's bed, while she complained that she had been abandoned: 'Returning from a whist drive, I found my husband gone and now he won't speak to me when he meets me at a whist drive or in the street.'[9] Such stories never seemed to go out of fashion. Sixty years later, the same newspaper carried a story under the headline, 'The final fling of a worried man'.

> At 52 Vincent Golden feared that his golden days were almost over. To his dismay he sensed the first signs of the dreaded 'male menopause' whose onset can mean that a man will no longer be the man he used to be.
>
> That, it was suggested yesterday, could be the only explanation for an extraordinary spell in his life when for six months he tried, with other people's money, to make up for time to be lost. To give him something to remember, the desperate Civil Servant embarked on his final fling ... with a younger woman.[10]

9. *Daily Mail*, 1 May 1925. Also *Sunday Graphic*, 13 October 1935; *Birmingham Mail*, 2 January 1960.

10. *Daily Mail*, 5 September 1985. Also H. Pickles, 'Decades Apart But Who's Counting?', *Woman's Journal*, December 1994.

Naturally, the press was much more interested when it was a celebrity who was caught up in the turmoil of middle age. In 1955, forty-year-old Orson Welles was reported to be about to marry a twenty-four-year-old Italian actress;[11] in 1970, forty-seven-year-old Dr Christiaan Barnard was challenged about his relationship with a nineteen-year-old woman. 'Don't make me laugh', he replied, 'Would I be enamoured of a girl the same age as my daughter, Deidre?'[12] Twenty-five years later, the *Sunday Times* reported gleefully on a whole series of celebrity affairs.

> Phil Collins, 43, face like a peanut, heart like a demolition ball, has fallen for Orianne Cevey, 22, face like a model – who knows about her heart? ...
>
> Richard Gere was recently spotted escorting the creamy-faced British model Laura Bailey – also 22, all fresh-faced and innocent ...
>
> Look at the mess graduate girlie Emily Barr, 22, made with that Tory MP, Hartley Booth, 47. She thought she was so sound writing for The Guardian, working in the House. She flirted without intent, intoxicated his mind, broke his heart.[13]

A few months later, the paper carried a lengthy interview with the writer Martin Amis. 'Phase one of his mid-life crisis', it claimed, 'was the breakup of his marriage to Antonia Phillips, an American, with whom he has two sons, Jacob and Louis. He went off with another American, Isabel Fonseca, a writer.' It was, the interviewer went on to explain, 'a multifaceted Mid-Life Crisis (MLC), a shuddering reassessment of the Amis existence in the face of mortality'.[14]

Indeed, the press began to speculate whether such difficulties were an integral part of growing older. 'Middle-age is danger time for marriages', announced the *Daily Mail* in 1965.[15] 'Most men, in the end, like little girls who are seen and not heard', explained the *Sunday Times* in 1994. 'Why have a full-grown handful of a woman when you can have the graduate girlie?'

11. *Daily Mail*, 2 May 1955.   12. *Daily Sketch*, 17 February 1970.
13. *Sunday Times*, 11 September 1994. Such stories were a staple of newspapers such as the *Sun*, the *People* and the *News of the World*. For recent examples, see *Sun*, 6 July 1995 (Patrick Mower), *News of the World*, 9 July 1995 (Tommy Steele), 17 September 1995 (Judge Anthony Thornton) and 29 October 1995 (Mick Jagger).
14. *Sunday Times*, 19 March 1995. Also *Guardian*, 2 May 1994, *News of the World*, 14 May 1995.
15. *Daily Mail*, 14 June 1965.

> The graduate girlie – no longer teenager, not yet adult, has long,
> luscious hair and legs to match. She has a neat waist and hard stomach.
> She is lively with her bosoms, but not over-confident in her opinions
> – she has not lived enough to fully grow them.[16]

Magazine and newspaper columnists were agreed that middle-aged
men seemed unable to resist the attractions of a younger woman.
Agony aunts provided their readers, both male and female, with a
curious mixture of warning and reassurance. 'Middle-aged men
often think they are in love with young girls', warned Mrs Eyles in
1935, 'but the attention rarely lasts long.'[17] 'Many a man goes
through this phase in middle-age', agreed Evelyn Home in 1960,
but if he really loves her, he should leave her for his wife and
children. 'When this fever is past you will be glad you did not, for
a temporary obsession, spoil the rest of your life.'[18] 'Turning 40'
brings out men's deep-seated doubts and insecurities, concluded
the *News of the World* in 1995, and they require a lot of reassurance
if they are not to fall victim to the male menopause.[19]

Unfortunately, such evidence, for all its prurient fascination, tells
us remarkably little about the scale and significance of marital disharmony among the middle aged. Were marriages really more at
risk in middle age than at other stages of the life cycle? Is it true
that middle-aged marriages – like other marriages – were more
likely to end in failure at the end of the century than they were at
the beginning?

The most obvious way to tackle these questions is by examining
the divorce statistics which, whatever their complications, have been
available in age-specific form since the beginning of the 1950s. They
show that marriages were less, rather than more, at risk in middle
age than they were at earlier stages of the life cycle, the mean age
of divorce hovering around 38–9 for men and three years younger
for women.[20] In fact, Figure 5.1 shows that divorce rates were highest when men and women were in their late twenties and thirties,
not their forties and fifties. It has been pointed out that 60 per

16. *Sunday Times*, 11 September 1994. See also 24 July 1994, 9 April 1995; *Guardian*, 15 March 1994, *Observer*, 15 January 1995.
17. *Woman's Way*, 9 February 1935. Also *Sunday Graphic*, 22 March, 3 May 1931.
18. *Woman*, 19 March 1960. Also 4 March 1950.
19. *News of the World*, 13 August 1995. Also *Sunday Mirror*, 26 March 1995; *Daily Mirror*, 8 October 1996; P. Lambley, *The Middle Aged Rebel*, Element Books, Shaftesbury, Dorset, 1995, p. 83.
20. Office of Population Censuses and Surveys, *Marriage and Divorce Statistics (England and Wales)*, HMSO, 1992, pp. 34–5, 50–1.

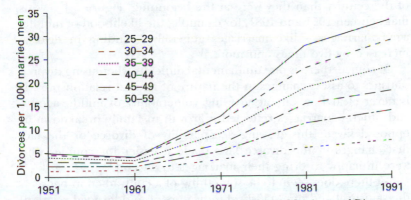

Sources: Office of Population Censuses and Surveys, *Marriage and Divorce Statistics: Historical Series of Statistics on Marriages and Divorces in England and Wales, 1837–1983*, HMSO, 1990, p. 117; Office of Population Censuses and Surveys, *Marriage and Divorce Statistics (England and Wales)*, HMSO, 1992, p. 50.

Figure 5.1   *Age and men's divorce rates, 1951–91*

cent of men, and 70 per cent of women who divorced did so before they reached the age of forty.[21]

The view that marriages were most at risk when husbands and wives were in their late twenties and thirties, rather than their forties and fifties, receives powerful reinforcement when it is remembered that divorce marked the culmination and not the beginning of marital disharmony. Although the time between things starting to go wrong, separation and the granting of a divorce decree obviously varied enormously, it could easily amount to six, seven years or more.[22] The marital disharmony that led to divorce most certainly tended to begin well before the onset of middle age.

It is also possible to use the age-specifc statistics of divorce to examine the extent to which middle-aged marriages became more vulnerable as the century wore on. When this is done, it confirms what common sense suggests: that middle-aged marriages – like marriages generally – were more likely to end in divorce at the end

21. Storr, 'New Life', p. 39; D. A. Coleman, 'Recent Trends in Marriage and Divorce in Britain and Europe', in R. W. Hiorns (ed.), *Demographic Patterns in Developed Societies*, Taylor and Francis, London, 1980, pp. 94, 97; N. Hart, *When Marriage Ends: A Study in Status Passage*, Tavistock, 1976, p. 77.
22. Hart, *When Marriage Ends*, p. 60; information from Jon Bernades.

of the century than they were at the beginning. Figure 5.1 reveals that between 1951 and 1981, for example, the likelihood of middle-aged marriages – like marriages generally – ending in divorce increased by five times and more.[23]

Of course, there is one fundamental difficulty when using divorce statistics to assess changes in the nature of marital relationships. It is never clear how far the growing vulnerability of middle-aged – and other – marriages reflected a growth in family breakdown as opposed say to the growing acceptability of divorce or the fact that changes in the divorce laws made it easier for couples who were unhappy to bring their marriages to an end.[24]

Yet there does seem to be something of a contradiction between the statistical and non-statistical indicators of middle-aged relationships. In fact, this contradiction is less profound than it appears at first sight. On the one hand, neither set of indicators is easy to interpret: many middle-aged (and other) couples lived together in unhappy, 'empty-shell' marriages without ever contemplating adultery; and many too committed adultery and went their separate ways without going anywhere near a divorce court.[25] On the other hand, it may be that the publicity afforded to middle-age adultery and divorce occurred not because such behaviour was common but because it was uncommon. It may be, in other words, that there was an inverse relationship between the popular perception and the private reality of marital disharmony in middle age.[26]

It follows, therefore, that two broad conclusions can be drawn. It seems certain that marriages were less vulnerable when husbands and wives were in their forties and fifties than when they were in their late twenties and thirties. It seems certain too that middle-aged marriages, like marriages generally, were a great deal more at risk at the end of the century than they had been at the beginning.

23. Between 1901 and 1991 the number of divorces in England and Wales increased from under 500 to almost 16,000. Office of Population Censuses and Surveys, *Divorce Statistics*, p. 50; Office of Population Censuses and Surveys, *Marriage and Divorce Statistics: Historical Series of Statistics on Marriages and Divorces in England and Wales, 1837–1983*, HMSO, 1990, p. 114.

24. Information from Jon Bernardes; R. Phillips, *Untying the Knot: A Short History of Divorce*, Cambridge University Press, Cambridge, 1991, ch. 9; E. Roberts, *Women and Families: An Oral History, 1940–1970*, Blackwell, Oxford, 1995, pp. 110–14.

25. Information from Jon Bernardes; Hart, *When Marriage Ends*, p. 60; J. R. Gillis, *For Better, For Worse: British Marriages 1600 to the Present*, Oxford University Press, Oxford, 1985, pp. 302–3.

26. See A. Lawson, *Adultery: An Analysis of Love and Respect*, Oxford University Press, Oxford, 1990, pp. 172–3.

Middle-aged parents and teenage children

Middle age was a traumatic time in parents' relationships with their children. Whether or not husbands and wives lived happily together, they usually experienced considerable difficulties in dealing with their teenage sons and daughters. However, once again, it is no easy matter to separate public rhetoric from private reality.

Nonetheless, there does seem to be incontrovertible evidence that middle-aged parents tended to have problems with their children. Such difficulties are not difficult to understand. As parents knew only too well – and as Figure 5.2 shows only too clearly – the early middle age of parents tended to coincide with the adolescence of their children.[27] So at the same time as parents were trying to cope with the first signs of ageing, their children were struggling to deal with the transition from childhood to adulthood. It was a volatile combination. 'Those years may coincide with a parent's declining years in sexual activity; teenagers peak while their parents fade.'[28]

Parents, it seemed, could argue with their children over virtually anything. They worried about their children's choice of friends, clothes and hair styles. They complained that their children made too much noise, did too little to help and stayed out far too late. They found it difficult to cope when their children asked them for money, and difficult too when they began to become financially independent.[29] Middle age, concluded comedian Jim Bowen in 1988, is when you have to work hard at maintaining social contact with your children.[30]

Some thought it best to be accommodating. A woman from Barrow-in-Furness recalls that as a thirteen-year-old school-leaver at the beginning of the century she became a drummer at the local skating rink: working afternoons and evenings she earned eighteen

27. J. C. Coleman, *Relationships in Adolescence*, Routledge & Kegan Paul, 1974, p. 68.
28. *Guardian*, 15 November 1995. Also *Lancet*, 23 October 1943; T. N. A. Jeffcoate, 'Drugs for Menopausal Symptoms', *British Medical Journal*, 30 January 1960; C. Ballinger, 'Psychiatric Morbidity and the Menopause: Screening of General Population Sample', *British Medical Journal*, 9 August 1975; T. K. Hareven, 'The Life Course and Ageing in Historical Perspective', in T. K. Hareven and K. J. Adams (eds), *Ageing and Life Course Transitions: An Interdisciplinary Perspective*, Tavistock, 1982.
29. *Sunday Graphic*, 8 March 1931; *Daily Sketch*, 27 February 1970; P. Thompson, *The Edwardians: The Remaking of British Society*, Paladin, 1977, p. 70; J. Benson, *The Rise of Consumer Society in Britain, 1880–1980*, Longman, 1994, ch. 7.
30. *Weekend*, 15 October 1988.

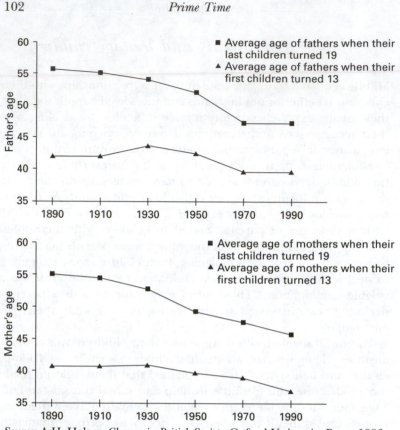

Source: A.H. Halsey, *Change in British Society*, Oxford University Press, 1986, p. 106.

Figure 5.2   *Changing age profile of the fathers and mothers of teenage children, 1890–1990. The census-based sample group in each case is of all parents who turned 40 in a given year*

shillings a week – only three shillings less than her father brought home from his job as a labourer. 'My mother used to let me have it easy in a morning, and some of the neighbours said, "Why don't you make you Carrie do this and that?" And my mother used to say, "I'm not going to kill the goose that lays the golden eggs".'[31] Others could not help but be resentful. It was revealed during the 1930s that 'many a father found his dignity and authority as the main

31. E. Roberts, *A Woman's Place: An Oral History of Working-class Women 1890–1940*, Blackwell, Oxford, 1984, p. 41.

support of a family replaced by a sense of ignominious dependence on the earnings of children, who sometimes resented the burden of the maintenance of their parents' home'.[32] It was discovered during the 1970s and 1980s that 'some men reach a final stage of becoming institutionalized in unemployment, with a sense of helplessness, futility and lack of control over their destiny', and that such reactions were particularly common among 'men in their middle years with family responsibilities who feel their role as the breadwinner diminished and their status in the household and society "demeaned" – a word often used'.[33]

It is a great deal more difficult to decide whether, and to what extent, parents' difficulties with their children intensified during the course of the century. On the one hand, there are reasons to suppose that certain aspects of economic, social and demographic development made it easier for middle-aged parents to deal with their teenage children. Parents were becoming more prosperous, more healthy and, it must not be forgotten, somewhat younger.[34] Figure 5.2 shows that at the beginning of the century parents had teenage children while they were in their forties and early to mid fifties, whereas a hundred years later they had them while they were in their late thirties and early to mid forties. This, it has been suggested, was a most crucial development, with younger parents supposedly finding it easier to deal with adolescent children.[35] Marry young, the *Sunday Graphic* advised its readers in 1935. 'The frank and easy companionship of a forty-year-old mother and an eighteen-year-old daughter, or of a father of forty-two and a son of twenty-one, can be and often is a very delightful relation[ship].'[36]

On the other hand, there are reasons for suggesting that certain aspects of demographic, economic and social development made it more difficult for the middle aged to relate to their children. 'At no time in our history have the generations been pitted against each other as they are now,' claimed Germaine Greer in 1992: 'households contain only parents and children and no representatives of intervening age groups, no young aunts and uncles,

32. Thompson, 'Problems'.

33. J. Burnett, *Idle Hands: The Experience of Unemployment, 1790–1990*, Routledge, 1994, pp. 289–90.

34. M. Anderson, 'The Emergence of the Modern Life Cycle in Britain', *Social History*, 10, 1985, p. 70.

35. Rossi, 'Life-span Theories', p. 25. Also Lambley, *Middle Aged Rebel*, p. 42.

36. *Sunday Graphic*, 17 November 1935.

no older cousins, and very few brothers and sisters'.[37] There were
other reasons besides.

> Britons who grew up in the depression years of the 1930s brought up
> children who took the boom years of the 1950s and 1960s for granted,
> but are now bringing up children to join the youth unemployment
> statistics of the 1980s. Such different experiences make for different
> assumptions and expectations about how society can and should work,
> and these differences may, in turn, be expressed in social conficts, in
> a 'generation gap'.[38]

Whatever the origins of the so-called generation gap, there was
a significant, long-term increase in public anxiety about the quality
of parent–child relationships. Levels of concern remained relatively
modest during the first thirty to forty years of the century. Mothers
of teenage daughters must realise that times have changed, warned
Woman's Way in 1935, but it was perfectly possible to adapt. 'Try
making a pal of your girl, and if you're the right kind of mother,
she'll want to make a pal of you!'[39]

Such solutions appeared almost comically inadequate in the face
of the economic, social and cultural changes that confronted parents during the second half of the century. It was widely believed
in the late 1940s that 'parents today are not as willing to sacrifice
personal comfort and pleasure in the interests of their children,
and that many children at the age of puberty or soon after lose all
sense of responsibility and affection for their family'.[40] It was suggested in the mid 1990s that the television comedy 'Absolutely
Fabulous' was less divorced from reality than might be imagined,
with middle-aged parents finding new and ever more embarrassing
ways of alienating their teenage children. 'Edina and Patsy could
have been modelled on my mother and her best friend', claimed
nineteen-year-old Sarah Burrows. 'Watching them stagger around
reminds me of times like when mum showed up at a birthday party
I gave, falling into the kitchen half-drunk, laughing and shouting,
making the room go quiet.'[41]

It seems therefore that popular perceptions about middle-aged
parents' relationships with their children were broadly correct.

37. G. Greer, *The Change: Women, Ageing and the Menopause*, Penguin, 1992, p. 38.
38. S. Frith, *The Sociology of Youth*, Causeway Books, Ormskirk, 1984, p. 6. Also
Lambley, *Middle Aged Rebel*, p. 42.
39. *Woman's Way*, 16 February 1935.   40. Thompson, 'Problems'.
41. *Observer*, 23 April 1995.

Whoever they were, wherever they lived and whenever they became middle-aged, many, if not most, couples experienced considerable difficulties in dealing with their teenage sons and daughters. Whoever they were, wherever they lived and whenever they became middle-aged, many, if not most, couples probably experienced more difficulties with their children towards the end of the century than their great grandparents did with theirs ninety or a hundred years before.

Middle-aged children and elderly parents

It is much less clear whether popular perceptions about the middle aged's neglect of the elderly were equally well founded. Although it is self-evident that it was the middle aged who had elderly parents and it can be shown that they did not always look after them as well as they might, it is a great deal more difficult to decide whether or not such neglect was common, let alone whether or not it intensified during the course of the century.

It was claimed time and time again that families – headed of course by the middle aged – were becoming increasingly neglectful of their parents. It was suggested that in the years following the First World War family cohesion and care for the sick and disabled were undermined by a complex combination of factors: long-term separation brought about by the war, unemployment, poor accommodation and overcrowding, the spread of divorce, the increase in female employment and, so it was said, the fact that domestic help was virtually unobtainable.[42] Such complaints became particularly insistent during and immediately following the establishment of the welfare state. According to the medical press, more and more of the elderly were ending up in institutional care: the *British Medical Journal* reported in 1949 that,

> It is the opinion of many with long experience of the work in institutions for the chronic sick and aged that the sense of family unity and responsibility is weakening, and that people in this country are less interested than they were in the fate of their elderly and disabled relatives.[43]

42. Thompson, 'Problems'.
43. Thompson, 'Problems'. Also M. O'Sullivan, 'The Problem of the Aged Sick as Seen by the General Practioner', *British Medical Journal*, 14 June 1952; Dr J. H. Sheldon cited in *British Medical Journal*, 31 July 1954.

But how seriously should such complaints be taken? Was there really a weakening of family ties, and did it really encourage the middle aged to abandon their elderly relatives to the uncertain mercies of institutional care?

Such questions are not at all easy to answer. It is well known of course that the growing number of old people, new patterns of family life and changing attitudes towards the role of the state meant that the care of the elderly came to assume new, and more compelling dimensions. It will be recalled from Chapter 2 that the twentieth century witnessed a most striking shift in the demographic balance between the middle aged and the elderly. Whereas in 1901 there were seven of the middle aged to two of the elderly, in 1981 there were only three of the former to two of the latter. This was a crucial development. It created profound and intractable problems not only for those charged with considering the public policy implications of an ageing population, but also for the thousands upon thousands of middle-aged couples struggling to decide how best to look after a bedridden aunt or an incontinent father.

Fortunately, it is possible to present a small amount of statistical data about the care of the elderly. It was reported in 1972 that 'The number of old people in public residential accommodation has multiplied by more than five since 1900 ... and since 1930 they have represented an increasing proportion of the age group'.[44] Here, it seems, is clear support for the view that family ties were weakening and middle-aged responsibilities falling into abeyance.

However, such a view would be most misleading. It is essential both to distinguish between absolute and relative levels of institutional care and to specify precisely which period it is that is being discussed. When this is done, it becomes clear that although the number of old people in public institutional care increased more than five times between 1900 and 1970, the percentage of the elderly population receiving such care declined by practically 40 per cent. It becomes clear too that there was a marked difference between different parts of the century: the proportion of old people in public institutional care declined by 75 per cent between 1900 and 1938, but increased by over 140 per cent between 1938 and 1980.[45]

44. J. Parker, 'Welfare', in A. H. Halsey (ed.), *Trends in British Society since 1900: A Guide to the Changing Social Structure of Britain*, Macmillan, Basingstoke, 1972, p. 465.
45. A. H. Halsey, (ed.), *British Social Trends since 1900: A Guide to the Changing Social Structure of Britain*, Macmillan, Basingstoke, 1988, p. 469.

So while it is impossible to use the numbers of old people in institutional care as evidence of consistent, long-term decline in family
concern, it is possible to use them to support the contention that
the establishment of the welfare state coincided with a diminution
of middle-aged support for elderly family members.

It remains difficult then to know how to assess the relationship
between middle-aged couples and their elderly relatives. Indeed,
such difficulty and contradiction is not uncharacteristic of the assessment generally of middle-aged relationships. Nevertheless, it is clear
that popular views of middle age as a time of crisis and maladjustment stand in need of substantial modification. This is not to deny
that such views had a certain validity: middle-aged parents had problems with their teenage children, and these problems tended to
increase during the course of the century. But other aspects of the
popular demonisation of middle-aged relationships had far less basis
in reality. Middle-age marriages were not particularly at risk and
the middle aged were never at all likely to place their parents in
institutional care.

Indeed, it is a great deal more difficult to generalise about middle-
aged relationships than even these contradictions and qualifications
suggest. Middle-aged relationships were as heterogeneous as any
others; they were characterised as much by difference and divergence
as they were by similarity and convergence. Not all the middle aged
were heterosexual, not all were married, not all had teenage children, and not all had parents to worry about.[46] Accordingly, it is the
purpose of the remainder of the chapter to show how hazardous it
is to generalise even about those living in conventional households.
This will be done in two ways. It will be shown that families survived,
stabilised and prospered – as well as disintegrated – during middle
age, and that the forties and fifties were years during which gender
differences – though not class differences – tended to assume still
greater significance than they did at earlier stages of the life cycle.

Pleasures and possibilities

It is easy to overlook the fact that many relationships proved resilient when confronted by the challenges of middle age. While there

---

46. R. Bacon, G. S. Bain and J. Pimlott, 'The Economic Environment', in Halsey
(ed.), *Trends*, pp. 76–7.

is no denying that marriages floundered, parents grew apart from their teenage children, and sons and daughters turned their backs on their elderly parents, it should not be assumed that such developments were typical – and it should certainly not be accepted that they can be used to describe, let alone to define, middle-aged relationships in all their complexity.

Most marriages survived, some stabilised and some prospered. Indeed, it is not difficult to show that, whatever the reason, the overwhelming majority of marriages survived well into middle age. Ninety-eight per cent of couples marrying in 1926, 94 per cent of those marrying in 1936 and 92 per cent of those marrying in 1951 had not divorced by the time they reached their late forties.[47] Of course, it is immeasurably more difficult to show that marriages remained strong, or grew stronger, in middle age. In fact, it may be tempting to dismiss such notions as fanciful, as little more than the sort of easy consolation dispensed by out-of-touch agony aunts in the pages of women's magazines.[48] Yet such reassurances should not be discounted out of hand. It was perfectly possible for marriages to improve when couples were in their forties and fifties. Forty-one-year-old Marilyn Johnson told *Woman's Own* in 1996 that her relationship with her husband Stephen had improved as they grew older.

> When you're young there's pressure to have sex as often as everybody else. This means sometimes you have sex when you don't want to, so it's disappointing. We don't do that anymore. Sex is more about love these days. I feel more for Stephen because we've grown up together.[49]

Parents' relationships with their children were equally heterogeneous. Even in the late 1950s and 1960s, when the new teenage culture caused such widespread concern, some middle-aged couples seemed to survive their children's adolescence with surprisingly little conflict and animosity. Some apparently welcomed the new fashions. 'Who's got my gloves, who wears my skirt?', demanded a young woman from Yeovil in 1960.

> My blouse, my coat, my jeans, my shirt?
> My shoes are gone, my belt's not there,

47. Coleman, 'Recent Trends', pp. 94–5; Office of Population Censuses and Surveys, *Historial Series*, pp. 90–4.
48. For example, *Woman*, 11 February 1950.
49. *Woman's Own*, 28 October 1995. Also B. Friedan, *The Fountain of Age*, Vintage, 1994, p. 246; M. Fiske, *Middle Age: The Prime of Life?*, Harper & Row, London, 1979, ch. 9.

My slip is back, flung on a chair;
It's not another teenage chum,
It is (just think) my sprightly Mum![50]

Other parents apparently found little fundamental with which to quarrel. Even in the 1960s, one in three teenagers attended evening classes and went to church regularly. In fact, when Mick Jagger and Keith Richards of the Rolling Stones were sentenced to imprisonment in 1967 following a massively publicised drugs trial, 85 per cent of teenagers interviewed in a National Opinion Poll either agreed with the sentence or wished to see it increased.[51] Care must be taken, then, not to exaggerate the scale and significance of middle age–teenage hostility. ' "Rebellious youth" and "the conflict between generations" are phrases that ring', conceded two expert commentators in 1966, 'but, so far as we can tell, it is not the ring of truth they carry so much as the beguiling but misleading tone of drama.'[52]

Moreover, it should be remembered that parent–child relationships often changed, and changed for the better between early middle age and late middle age. Yet such an improvement is easily missed, with the connotations placed upon the so-called 'empty-nest' syndrome obscuring the fact that children leaving home could be a cause of relief as well as regret.

The empty nest is commonly seen as one of the two great crises of women's lives.[53] As members of the medical profession liked to explain, 'when the children mature and leave home the mother may be left without any self-satisfying interests and lives a bored and aimless existence'.[54] As women's magazines never tired of pointing out, whether or not mothers had 'self-satisfying interests', it was only natural for them to miss their children.

At the age of 43, I was losing my identity. I was no longer the mother of children. Night after night, I'd dream I was back when the children were small. One minute I'd be baking mince pies in the kitchen with the girls playing at my feet and I'd be filled with all the old

50. Miss E. R. to *Woman*, 2 January 1960.
51 . J. Ryder and H. Silver, *Modern English Society: History and Structure 1850–1970*, Methuen, 1970, p. 261.
52. Coleman, *Relationships in Adolescence*, p. 69. Also pp. 73–4; *Woman*, 25 February 1950.
53. The other of course is the menopause. S. Bovey, *The Empty Nest*, Pandora/HarperCollins, 1995.
54. Jeffcoate, 'Drugs'.

feelings of contentment. Then I would wake up and the loss would hit me all over again.[55]

Indeed, even agony aunt Virginia Ironside admitted in 1994 that she faced feelings of profound grief and loss when her son went to India and started at university. 'Parenting is all about loss. My advice is to acknowledge the way you are feeling and talk about it with your partner.'[56]

Nonetheless, the connection that is commonly made between middle age, the empty nest and feelings of parental loss needs to be approached with considerable caution. While it is true that parents tended to be middle-aged when their children left home, they were more likely to be in their late forties and fifties than in their early forties. So although it is difficult to determine precisely parents' ages when their children moved elsewhere, husbands and wives were usually in their late forties when their eldest sons went to university and in their mid to late fifties when they got married.[57] It seems therefore that the association between middle age and the empty nest should be reformulated more accurately – and more helpfully – as the association between late middle age and the empty nest.

However, it does not follow that late middle-aged parents necessarily suffered an abrupt sense of loss when their children left home. Most couples had more than one child so that they experienced the empty nest not as a single event but as a process which occurred over several years. Moreover, many husbands and wives apparently regarded the empty nest as a source of relief as well as – or rather than – a source of regret. It has been claimed, for example, that 'for most married couples the maturing of children and their departure from the home is a liberating experience giving couples who can expect many more years of life time to think about their lives and how the future will be filled'.[58] 'I'm 50 and my sex life is better now than it's ever been before', claimed Jean Maher in 1996. 'And having the house to ourselves is like being on a second honeymoon.'[59]

Whether or not the empty nest strengthened late middle-aged marriages, many couples found that it enabled them to re-establish

55. *Woman's Realm*, 25 January 1994. Also *Woman*, 8 January 1938; *Woman's Realm*, 30 January 1960; *Woman's Weekly*, 2 July 1996.

56. *Woman's Realm*, 25 January 1994.

57. Office of Population Censuses and Surveys, *Historical Series*, pp. 89–91; A. H. Halsey, *Change in British Society*, Oxford University Press, Oxford, 1986, p. 106.

58. M. Hepworth and M. Featherstone, *Surviving Middle Age*, Blackwell, Oxford, 1982, p. 45. Also Lambley, *Middle Aged Rebel*, p. 42.

59. *Woman's Own*, 28 October 1996.

their relationships with their children on new and more secure foundations. When their children left home, it removed many of the day-to-day irritations of living together. So even if the children did not move far away or came back frequently on visits, many parents were pleased to have the house to themselves: they enjoyed not having to queue for the bathroom, not having to be quiet in the mornings – and not being woken up late at night.[60] Moreover, the rites of passage that marked early adulthood provided public opportunities for children to articulate the ties that bound them to their middle-aged parents. A Preston man recalls proudly the day that his son got married. 'And in his wedding day speech, he turned round and he said, "And what I have today, I owe to my father". And to me that was like Littlewoods presenting me with a cheque.'[61]

There is other evidence too that late middle age saw the strengthening of parent–child relationships. Change was inevitable and welcome, believed some.[62] Bernice Andrews and George Brown concluded their detailed psychological investigation of a hundred north London women during the 1980s with some highly pertinent comments on the relationship between middle age, motherhood and self-esteem.

> The middle years for women have often been considered a difficult time when issues bound up with loss of youth and fertility need to be faced. The role of primary care-giver can be lost with the meaning and sense of self it can bring. However, as children grow older there are potential advantages. . . . A number of women were getting on better with their children – many who had been very difficult in early adolescence had settled down and had become sources of support and companionship.[63]

It should come as no surprise either to discover that relationships between the middle aged and their parents were probably as heterogeneous as those between the middle aged and their children. When the children of the middle aged became middle-aged in their turn, many of them tried very hard to support their now elderly parents.

It is simply not true that those in their forties and fifties did little more than dump their elderly relative in the nearest institution

60. Personal recollection; *Woman's Own*, 28 October 1996.
61. University of Lancaster, 'Family and Social Life in Barrow, Lancaster and Preston 1940–1970', Mr 5NP, p. 30.
62. Wolverhampton Oral History Project (hereafter WOH), Mrs B.
63. B. Andrews and G. W. Brown, 'Stability and Change in Low Self-esteem: The Role of Psychosocial Factors', *Psychological Medicine*, 26, 1995, pp. 7–8.

that would accept them. Some looked after their parents no matter what the financial and social cost.[64] Only a tiny minority of old people were ever placed in any sort of public institutional care: surveys carried out in 1908 and 1977 suggest that no more than one per cent of old people with close surviving relatives were to be found in institutional care.[65] Nor is it true that once in care, the elderly were promptly forgotten by their middle-aged sons and daughters. What little evidence there is suggests that children made considerable efforts to visit their parents. In 1949, the *British Medical Journal* carried a detailed report on elderly patients in Birmingham's Western Road Infirmary. It revealed that during the first three months of their stay, 82 per cent of men and 79 per cent of women were visited at least once a week, and that even after four years in care, 40 per cent of men and 46 per cent of women were still receiving at least one visit a week.[66]

Then too a surprisingly large number of middle-aged children had their parents to live with them. In fact, it seems that during the first half of the century it may have become more, rather than less, common for sons and daughters to help their mothers and fathers in this way. The combination of increasing longevity and declining family size meant that as time went by, there were more elderly parents to care for but fewer middle-aged children to do so.[67] It has been calculated that in 1951, for example, at least 40 per cent of those aged sixty and over – and probably 60 per cent of those with surviving children – were to be found living with a son or daughter.[68]

Sometimes co-residence worked well. A fifty-one-year-old personnel officer from Lancaster reported in 1988 that he and his wife had her mother living with them. They all ate together but his mother-in-law had her own room: 'Which is ideal really, we don't have any problems of any nature it all works out quite well really.'[69] However, co-residence often exacerbated rather than alleviated domestic difficulties. A 1948 survey of old people in Wolverhampton revealed that a significant proportion of those caring for elderly relatives reported that it placed them under considerable strain.

64. WOH, Mr Q.
65. Roberts, *Women and Families*, p. 197; Thompson, 'Problems'. Also Editorial in *British Medical Journal*, 6 August 1949; J. H. Sheldon, 'The Role of the Aged in Modern Society', *British Medical Journal*, 11 February 1950.
66. Thompson, 'Problems'.   67. Roberts, *Woman's Place*, p. 175.
68. P. Townsend, *The Family Life of Old People: An Inquiry in East London*, Routledge & Kegan Paul, 1957, pp. 21–2. Also J. Fry, 'Care of the Elderly in General Practice: A Socio-Medical Reassessment', *British Medical Journal*, 21 September 1957.
69. 'Family and Social Life', Mr G3L, p. 61.

Forty-four per cent of the sample found the old person difficult to deal with, 35 per cent felt that they had too much to do, 49 per cent reported that they were unable to go out as much as they wished, and 29 per cent complained that it was impossible for them to get away on holiday.[70] The Carnegie Inquiry into the Third Age concluded with remarkable restraint in 1992 that, 'Although caring brings some satisfaction, and is often undertaken willingly, this satisfaction is nearly always outweighed by serious problems' both financial and psychological. 'Daughters who provide care seem more prone to psychological problems than spouse or other carers.'[71]

It was more common for middle-aged children to live near to, and help, their elderly parents. Nor should it be supposed that such residential proximity and filial support were the preserve of the unskilled and poorly paid. Indeed, one of the reasons that Wolverhampton was chosen for the 1948 survey of old people was that its size meant that there was no difficulty 'in obtaining a random sample giving access to every income-group from rich to poor'.[72] The investigation revealed that 4 per cent of old people in the town had children near by, 10 per cent had children in the same street, and 20 per cent had children within half a mile.[73]

A widower aged 70 lives by himself, but his midday meal is cooked by a daughter living in the same street. In case of illness one of his 3 daughters, all of whom live close, would come and stay with him, while her own family would be cared for by her 2 sisters.

A widow aged 70 lives by herself. She habitually spends the day with a married daughter living in the same street and helps to look after the grandchidren, which she greatly enjoys and at which she is very useful. She only uses her own home for bed and breakfast. In case of illness, of either the subject or the daughter, each would look after the other.[74]

Such patterns of proximity and support proved vulnerable to the demographic, economic and ideological changes which occurred during the second half of the century. It was not just that new patterns of fertility, growing geographical mobility, the expansion of female employment and new attitudes towards the role of the

70. J. H. Sheldon, *The Social Medicine of Old Age: Report of an Inquiry in Wolverhampton*, Nuffield Foundation, 1948, pp. 181–3.
71. Carnegie Inquiry into the Third Age, *Caring: The Importance of Third Age Carers*, Carnegie Trust, 1992, p. ix.
72. Sheldon, *Social Medicine*, p. 3.
73. Sheldon, 'Role'. Also Townsend, *Family Life*, p. 31ff.
74. Sheldon, *Social Medicine*, pp. 152–3. Also *British Medical Journal*, 27 May 1961; editorial, 6 August 1959.

state disrupted existing family-based systems of support.[75] It was
also that improving health, growing longevity, increasing prosperity, the convenience of central heating, the spread of consumer
durables and the company provided by radio and television enabled
old people to sustain their independence longer than had been
possible in earlier years.[76]

Men and women, children and parents

Nor is this by any means the end of the matter. As was suggested
above, the difficulties of generalising about middle-aged relationships are compounded by the fact that middle age was a period during which gender differences tended to assume greater significance
than they did at earlier stages of the life cycle.

In fact, gender differences are absolutely fundamental to any
understanding of middle-aged relationships. For as a moment's
reflection will suggest, the ways in which men and women related to
their partners, their children and their parents were scarcely likely
to be the same. However, such differences are easily missed, and
the fact that men's and women's experiences tended to diverge,
rather than converge, in middle age seems often to be overlooked
amidst the increasingly common – and curiously compelling – demonisation of the middle years.

Men's and women's experiences of marriage most certainly
tended to diverge in middle age. This can be seen most obviously
by a reworking of the divorce statistics which were considered earlier in the chapter. There were two broad developments: the gap
between men's and women's divorce rates grew wider in middle
age, and grew wider still during the second half of the century. For
example, in 1951 men in their fifties were 23 per cent more likely
than women of the same age to get divorced; forty years later they
were 29 per cent more likely to do so.[77]

However, such statistics conceal – or at least do little to reveal –
more deep-seated differences between men's and women's experiences of middle-aged marriage. Husbands of all ages were more
likely than their wives to have affairs, and middle-aged husbands

75. Anderson, 'Modern Life Cycle', p. 75; WOH, Mr Q.
76. Roberts, *Women and Families*, pp. 190–8.
77. Office of Population Censuses and Surveys, *Historical Series*, p. 117; Office of
Population, Censuses and Surveys, *Marriage and Divorce Statistics*, p. 50.

were a great deal more likely than middle-aged wives to do so. So despite the prurient attention that was paid to affairs between middle-aged women and younger men,[78] it was middle-aged men, and not middle-aged women, who were likely to be unfaithful.[79] As a leading figure in the Conservative party explained in 1995 in a breathtaking combination of ageism, sexism and class prejudice, 'At 40 ... you drop your trousers ... and run off with the secretary'.[80]

Of course, it is much more difficult to generalise about middle-aged marriages than the discussion of adulterous husbands and betrayed wives would lead one to suppose. While it is true that men's and women's experiences of marriage tended to diverge in middle age, they did so in ways that were a good deal more complicated than conventional analysis and popular stereotyping tend to suggest.

Middle-aged women, like women generally, began to develop higher expectations of marriage. The key to this change lay, it has been suggested, in the growing numbers of married women who were working outside the home. The proportion of married women between thirty-five and forty-four who were recorded as economically active grew prodigiously in the years following the Second World War: from some 10 per cent between 1911 and 1931, to 25 per cent or so in 1951, and well over 60 per cent in 1981.[81] It was this expansion of married women's employment, believes Penny Summerfield, 'which provided a margin of economic independence sufficient to give women the confidence to dissolve a marriage that was not living up to expectations'.[82]

It also gave them the confidence to challenge the assumptions upon which their marriages were based. In all events, the fear of the economically independent and sexually emancipated middle-aged woman had deep roots. 'One school of thought held that women became amoral at menopause, because their sexuality was liberated from its reproductive function and became like a man's.'[83] If few observers felt that middle-aged women became immoral, many came to believe that middle age precipitated a shift in the domestic balance of power. As agony aunt Evelyn Home explained in 1958,

78. *Observer*, 15 January 1995; *Daily Mail*, 4 September 1995; *News of the World*, 17 September 1995.
79. Lawson, *Adultery*, p. 78.   80. *Guardian*, 10 May 1995.
81. Halsey (ed.), *British Social Trends*, p. 172.
82. P. Summerfield, 'Women in Britain since 1945: Companionate Marriage and the Double Burden', in Obelkevich and Catterall, *British Society*, p. 67. Also Lawson, *Adultery*, pp. 186–7; *Daily Mail*, 4 May 1996.
83. Greer, *The Change*, p. 103.

men often found work more difficult as they grew older, but women probably found housework easier as their children grew into teenagers and young adults.[84]

It is difficult, as so often, to distinguish the rhetoric from the reality. However, it does seem that the combination of increasing longevity, declining family size, expanding employment and the burgeoning women's movement encouraged middle-aged women to look anew at their marriages. Many of them did not like what they saw. In 1975 the *Daily Mail* carried a feature on 'The 40 Year Itch' that sought to explain 'why so many wives are now walking out'.

> For generations, the idea that 'Life begins at 40' was reserved for men. Life ended at 40 for women, with a stay of execution only for those anointed few such as Jackie Onassis . . .
> That scenario has suddenly changed for women who used to fantasise in terror that their 40-year old husbands would leave them for someone younger.
> The new fantasy is for the 40-year old wife to say: 'John, I'm leaving in 15 minutes. Take care of yourself, I'll call in six months!' . . .
> While most over-40 men leave their wives for someone else, women of that age leave their husbands for something else.[85]

A few years later, a national survey of men aged between 25 and 35 voted middle-aged actress Joan Collins the country's foremost sex symbol. Asked about the secret of her success, she contrasted the ways in which men and women reacted to the ageing process. 'A lady in her forties has more to offer than just pretty physical packaging', she believed. 'Trying to be sexy doesn't come from wearing a short skirt or letting your boobs hang out. It comes from inside.' However, as she went on to explain, most men found it difficult to match this sense of inner energy once they reached the age of forty: they became complacent and did not seem to care whether their hair was a mess or whether they developed a pot belly.[86]

Men's and women's relationships with their children also tended to develop in contrasting ways during middle age. Women, it seems, reacted less well than men to the difficulties of the teenage years. Indeed, it has been suggested that there was a correlation not just between middle age and psychological illness but also between motherhood, middle age and psychological illness. A 1975 report on the health and ill-health of 40–55-year-old women concluded

---

84. *Woman*, 6 September 1958.
85. *Daily Mail*, 4 September 1975. Also 4 May 1996.
86. Hepworth and Featherstone, *Surviving Middle Age*, p. 27.

rather chillingly that 'Environmental factors, particularly in relation to children, seemed to be associated with increased psychiatric morbidity at this time of life'.[87]

Men and women also reacted differently to the empty nest. However, they did so in ways that were less straightforward than might be anticipated. Women who did not work outside the home often found it more difficult than their husbands to cope when their children began to live independently.[88] Many women, whether or not they worked outside the home, found, much more than their husbands, that the empty nest provided them with the opportunity for fulfilment and self-development.

> The empty nest brings about a shift in the power structure of the couple. It may allow the woman greater freedom for the first time: to enter higher education, a career, and this at a time when the husband's prospects may be diminishing and he has to come to terms with the fact that he may never realise his ambitions.[89]

Two academic psychologists explained in the mid 1990s that,

> as children grow older, there are potential advantages. . . . A number of women were getting on better with their children. . . . Some had given up the expectation of forming a satisfactory opposite-sex relationship and were gaining more satisfaction from their own employment and watching their children do well.[90]

Whether middle-aged women derived any satisfaction from watching their parents grow old is much more open to question. Duty struggled with exhaustion, regret with resentment. However, there is no denying that it was daughters, much more than sons, who had to learn how to cope with this range of conflicting emotions. 'How often have you seen the fifty-year-old woman guiding the seventy-five-year-old around the hospital, the supermarket, the theatre foyer?', demanded Germaine Greer.

> You will not often see a grandchild [or a fifty-year-old man] performing this labour of love; the middle-aged women are the only ones free to do it, and the whole responsibility tends to fall on them.[91]

---

87. Ballinger, 'Psychiatric Morbidity'.
88. *Sunday Graphic*, 1 February 1931; *Woman's Realm*, 25 January 1994; Bovey, *Empty Nest*; S. Bovey, 'Home Alone – For Mothers', *Guardian*, 8 November 1995.
89. Hepworth and Featherstone, *Surviving Middle Age*, p. 46.
90. Andrews and Brown, 'Stability and Change', p. 8. Also Friedan, *Fountain of Age*, p. 108.
91. Greer, *The Change*, p. 315. Also Consumers' Association, *Living Through Middle Age*, pp. 100–2.

The gendered nature of caring has a long history. The 1948 report on old age in Wolverhampton discovered thirty-seven cases in which 'the younger generation were carrying excessive strain in looking after old people'. All but one of these carers were women: twenty-eight daughters, six daughters-in-law, two nieces and one friend.[92]

> A daughter has the care of her father, in addition to that of her husband and child and boarder; the father has an overflow incontinence from an enlarged prostate. Living close by she has a mother-in-law, who has a senile mental failure with some incontinence of both urine and faeces. She does the large amount of washing that inevitably comes from both subjects, in addition to running her own house. When I called on a Saturday afternoon she was washing, and said she was always washing. She can hardly get out for pleasure, and has had no holiday for years.[93]

Thirty years later, the Consumers' Association confirmed the gendered inequality inherent in middle-aged caring, but tried desperately to be positive.

> A problem facing many middle-aged women and a comparatively small number of men on their own, is the care of infirm or elderly relatives at home . . .
> To those who spend many years caring for the old at home, there comes the difficult time when they are left alone and have to readjust their whole life . . .
> The spinster who has stayed at home to care for her parents may now feel that her life has been thrown away, but if she can have the courage to accept that she has missed certain elements, she can now look for different outlets and interests.[94]

Working-class responsibilities and middle-class opportunities

Class differences too are fundamental to the understanding of middle-aged relationships. For as a moment's reflection will suggest, the middle class and working class were no more likely than men

92. Sheldon, *Social Medicine*, p. 183.
93. Sheldon, *Social Medicine*, p. 184. Also Consumers' Association, *Living Through Middle Age*, pp. 100–2.
94. Consumers' Association, *Living Through Middle Age*, pp. 100, 102. Also Carnegie Inquiry, *Caring*, pp. 8–15.

and women to relate in identical ways to their partners, their children and their parents. Thus it is the purpose of the remainder of the chapter to explore the relationship between age, class and family relationships. It will be suggested that although class differences were always an important determinant of middle-aged relationships, they tended, if anything, to become less powerful during the course of the century.

There was a clear, albeit declining, correlation between class and marriage. This can be seen most clearly in terms of divorce. Although the divorce statistics considered earlier in the chapter cannot be reworked on a class basis, there is no doubt that for many years cost alone prevented working people of any age from even contemplating the possibility of ending their marriages in this way.[95] However, as working-class incomes rose and the cost of divorce declined, the proportion – and number – of working-class divorces increased dramatically.

> Between two sample years, 1871 and 1951, manual workers increased their representation in divorces from 22 to 69%, farmers and shop-keepers declined from 16 to 8%, while the higher social groups (gentry, professionals, and managers) plummeted from 54 to 16%.[96]

There was a clear, and apparently continuing, correlation between class and adultery. Despite the obvious empirical difficulties of studying an issue as private and elusive as marital infidelity, it seems clear that whatever their age, those from the middle class were more likely than those from the working class to engage in extramarital affairs. The Royal Commission on Divorce was told time and again in 1912 that there was less adultery among the poor than among the rich.[97] The National Survey of Sexual Attitudes and Lifestyles concluded in 1994 that there was a clear correlation between age, gender, class and adultery. 'Men over 45 in social classes I and II were more likely to report multiple partners in the last year than those in social classes IV and V.'[98] The *Sunday Times* put it rather less dispassionately:

95. *Royal Commission on Divorce and Matrimonial Causes*, 1912, II, Q. 12,305, W. J. Grubbe; Q. 13, 814, W. C. Williams; C. Chinn, *They Worked All Their Lives: Women of the Urban Poor in England, 1990–1939*, Manchester University Press, Manchester, 1988, p. 158; Phillips, *Untying the Knot*, p. 236.
96. Phillips, *Untying the Knot*, p. 239.
97. For example, *R. C. Divorce*, 1912, II, Q. 12,643, J. V. Austin.
98. K. Wellings, J. Field, A. M. Johnson and J. Wadsworth, *Sexual Behaviour in Britain: The National Survey of Sexual Attitudes and Lifestyles*, Penguin, 1994, p. 108. Also p. 249.

even in the heady throes of romance we – or rather, *men* – are bound
by the shackles of class. High-earning, professional men are five times
more likely to commit adultery than manual workers, and are more
unfaithful the older they get.[99]

It is not difficult to see why the relationship between age, gender,
class and adultery should prove so enduring. It was middle-aged,
middle-class men who were most likely to have the time, the money
and the opportunity to engage in affairs. A county court judge from
Bristol told the Royal Commission on Divorce in 1912 that,

> There is very much more temptation to a man who has money and
> more or less leisure than there is to the artisan who has very little
> money and very little leisure, and has to work very hard . . .
>   People do not go to country houses for week-ends amongst the
> poorer classes.[100]

The *Sunday Times* pointed out to its readers eighty years later, that
the explanation put forward by the National Survey of Sexual Attitudes and Lifestyles – that 'professional men have more opportunities, more money and a wider circle of friends – does ring true,
and the adulterers one could name fit the picture of well-to-do professional men'.[101]

Women's attitudes too were conditioned by their class. In fact, it
will not have escaped the reader's attention that the examples given
earlier in the chapter of middle-aged women's growing expectations of marriage had a distinctly middle-class feel to them. These
were women, it will be recalled, who saw the empty nest less as a
loss than as an opportunity to enter higher education or to further
their career aspirations. Yet it is important not to be misled, for
even towards the end of the century there were sharp differences
between middle-class and working-class attitudes towards the ageing process. Working-class women remained wedded much more
closely than middle-class women to the view that the responsibilities
of early adulthood would be followed, all too soon, by the inescap-
able deterioration which accompanied middle age.[102]

   The ways in which middle-aged parents related to their children
also tended to differ according to their class position. Indeed, the

99. *Sunday Times*, 9 April 1995.
100. *R. C. Divorce*, 1912, II, Q. 12,736–7, J. W. Austin.
101. *Sunday Times*, 9 April 1995.
102. Hepworth and Featherstone, *Surviving Middle Age*, p. 47. Also R. Hoggart,
*The Uses of Literacy: Aspects of Working-class Life with Special Reference to Publications and
Entertainments*, Penguin, 1958, pp. 41, 50, 54.

supposedly close-knit nature of the early twentieth-century working-class family serves as a well known and powerful symbol of the world we have lost: these were the years, we are told, in which families were friendly with their neighbours, left their doors unlocked at night, knew how to talk to their adolescent children and did their best to look after their elderly relatives.[103]

The truth, as so often, is a good deal more complicated, Although middle-aged parents from both the middle class and working class were able – in their different ways – to exercise a significant degree of economic control over their adolescent children, working-class parents seemed to find it easier to persuade their sons and daughters to continue to accept the values and standards with which they had been brought up.

It is a pity of course that so little attention has been paid to the history of the middle-class family. Nonetheless, the economic control of middle-aged, middle-class parents over their adolescent (and young adult) children can scarcely be doubted. Middle-class parents encouraged their children to stay on at school, discouraged them from taking on part-time work, supported them through university, and sometimes did what they could to help them buy a house or set themselves up in business.[104]

However, this continuing economic power often co-existed alongside a declining moral and ideological authority. Middle-class children were usually well educated and often moved some distance from their parents in order to study or to work, and this brought them into contact with a wider variety of ideas, attitudes and beliefs than working-class children who were more likely to stay close to the parental home. This sometimes exacerbated the difficulty which middle-class parents experienced in coping with the empty nest. The advice they received was not always terribly helpful. A reader of the *Sunday Graphic* was told in 1931 that 'Probably another mother whose birds have flown the nest would be glad of your companionship'. Or perhaps 'you know some lonely business girls who would be happy to be asked occasionally to the evening meal you used to prepare for your own young folk'.[105]

The history of the working-class family has received a great deal more attention. This shows, *inter alia*, that working-class parents continued to maintain a surprising degree of control – both material

103. J. Benson, *The Working Class in Britain, 1850–1939*, Longman, 1989, p. 117.
104. P. Thompson, *The Edwardians: The Remaking of British Society*, Paladin, 1977, p. 90; Benson, *Consumer Society*, pp. 66–7.
105. *Sunday Graphic*, 1 February 1931.

and ideological – over children whom one might have expected to
display a considerable amount of personal autonomy. Although
many working-class parents encouraged their children to work part-
time while at school, and to leave school as soon as possible to take
up full-time employment, they tried hard to discourage other signs
of independence. Robert Roberts recalls that in early twentieth-
century Salford,

> Teenagers, especially girls, were kept on a very tight rein. Fathers fixed
> the number of evenings on which they could go out and required
> to know precisely where and with whom they had spent their leisure.
> He set, too, the exact hour of their return; few dared to break their
> rule. One neighbour's daughter, a girl of nineteen, was beaten for
> coming home ten minutes late after choir practice.[106]

Oral historian Elizabeth Roberts agrees that it was 'unusual to find
much real independence, still less youthful rebellion'.[107] The 'truly
independent working-class youth, male or female, cannot be found
in any significant numbers' before the Second World War. For as
she goes on to explain, one must never overlook 'the immense *moral*
authority which parents continued to wield, and the great respect
their children continued to show well into adult life, in most cases
until the death of the parents'.[108]

> Such parental authority was undermined less than might be expected
> in the years following the Second World War. As I have argued
> elsewhere, the fact is that most young people, boys as well as girls,
> working-class as well as middle-class, rebelled a good deal more cau-
> tiously than a litany of . . . panics [about youthful behaviour] would
> lead one to suppose. The great majority of young people spent more
> time in their bedrooms or at church youth clubs than they did at
> rock festivals or on the football terraces. The great majority of young
> people managed to get through their teenage years without becom-
> ing involved in anything that could remotely – or at least reasonably
> – be described as deviant or delinquent behaviour.[109]

However, the most powerful element of public nostalgia for the
early twentieth-century working-class family centres around the care
that it is supposed to have devoted to the sick and the elderly. But
how far is such nostalgia justified? Was there really a difference

---

106. R. Roberts, *The Classic Slum: Salford Life in the First Quarter of the Century*,
Pelican, 1973, p. 51. Cf. Hoggart, *Literacy*, p. 53.
107. E. Roberts, 'The Family', in J. Benson (ed.), *The Working Class in England*,
1875–1914, Croom Helm, 1984, p. 26. Also p. 27.
108. Roberts, *Woman's Place*, p. 42.   109. Benson, *Consumer Society*, p. 168.

between the ways in which middle-class and working-class families looked after their old people? The answer seems to be that such nostalgia is based upon reasonably secure empirical foundations. Although it is easy to exaggerate the quality of the care that was offered in working-class families, it would be difficult to deny that middle-aged couples from even the most disadvantaged backgrounds often made strenuous efforts to support their parents as they grew older and less able to look after themselves.

Unfortunately, the comparison between working-class and middle-class care is not easily made. Middle-class care was likely to be private, individual and impersonal and thus impervious to detailed historical analysis. But this does not mean that it should be discounted. It was seen earlier in the chapter that professional couples sometimes did what they could to help the older generation. It can be shown just occasionally that such support was more common than the emphasis placed upon working-class solidarity would lead one to suppose. A 1957 investigation into the care of the elderly in a 'typical' London suburban general practice reported that 37 per cent of those in their seventies, and 50 per cent of those in their eighties, lived with family members. In fact, 86 per cent of those over seventy, it was discovered, maintained 'regular contact with their families'.[110]

Working-class care has always tended to arouse a great deal more interest. The investigations carried out into working people's support of the elderly make it clear, not surprisingly, that there were cases of cruelty and neglect.[111] However, these investigations suggest too that such cases were highly unusual. So despite the obvious dangers of lapsing into an idealised, romanticised vision of working-class warmth, loyalty and solidarity, it really does seem that during the first half of the century many working-class couples did what they could to support their elderly parents. Elizabeth Roberts concludes from her oral history of working-class women between 1890 and 1940 that it was common for middle-aged couples to have elderly parents to live with them or, most often, to visit them regularly in their own homes.[112] Peter Townsend reported in his classic 1957 study of old people in Bethnal Green, that 38 per cent of those over sixty lived with their children, and that most of the rest kept in frequent touch: 'two-thirds saw at least one of their daughters every

110. J. Fry, 'Care of the Elderly in General Practice: A Socio-Medical Reassessment', *British Medical Journal*, 21 September 1957.
111. Roberts, *Woman's Place*, pp. 170, 179.
112. Roberts, *Woman's Place*, p. 175.

day and nearly half one of their sons. Although 15% had no child within a mile, only 4% did not see at least one of their children once a week.'[113]

It is only too easy then to misrepresent the family relationships of the middle aged. Yet it is important not to be misled by prevailing perceptions of the ways in which those in their forties and fifties related to their partners, their children and their parents. If the family relationships of the middle aged were not always easy, they were marked by stability as well as by instability. Middle age, it must be remembered, was a period of advance and adaptability as well as of crisis and catastrophe.

113. Townsend, *Family Life*, pp. 21, 37.

CHAPTER SIX

Attitudes

Perhaps the most persistent of all beliefs about middle age has been that it was the time of life when attitudes tended to change – to change significantly, and to change almost always for the worse. Sometimes, it is conceded, the middle aged began to seek change and excitement.[1] But most often, it is believed, they began to hanker after security and stability, they grew censorious and conservative, they became distrustful of the younger generation, and they worried more and more about age and the signs of ageing.[2]

It is a dispiriting picture, and it is the purpose of this chapter to discover whether or not it is true. Its aim more specifically is to decide whether, and to what extent, the biological, psychological, material and other developments discussed in earlier chapters brought about – or reflected – changes in the ways that the middle aged viewed themselves and the world in which they lived.

These are complex issues. Not only is the study of ideas and attitudes always exceptionally difficult,[3] but the assessment of age-specific ideas and attitudes presents problems all of its own. These make it necessary, still more than in earlier chapters, to distinguish rigorously between age and generation. Unless every effort is made to compare the attitudes of the same generation – rather than of different generations – in adulthood and middle age, what appears to be a change in attitudes between adulthood and middle age may be no more than a change in attitudes between the adults of one generation and the middle aged of the preceding one. The assessment of age-specific ideas and attitudes demands, in other words,

---

1. A. Storr, 'A New Life in Middle Age', in R. Owen (ed.), *Middle Age*, BBC, 1967, p. 40; P. Drabble, *A Voice: The Wilderness*, Pelham, London, 1991, pp. 88–90.
2. For example, *Lancet*, 13 May 1913; *Wolverhampton Select Magazine*, August 1994.
3. J. Benson, *The Working Class in Britain, 1850–1939*, Longman, 1989, p. 141.

that as in any form of life-cycle analysis, evidence needs to be collected and analysis undertaken on a longitudinal rather than a cross-sectional basis.

When this is done, it becomes apparent that middle-aged attitudes were more heterogeneous than is generally supposed. It is true that people often tended to become more anxious, more conservative and more resentful when they reached their forties and fifties. Yet it would be a gross error to assume that the entire twentieth-century population, indigenous and immigrant, religious and non-religious, heterosexual and homosexual, male and female, working-class and middle-class, reacted in the same way to the onset of middle age. Middle age, it will be suggested, should be associated with divergence as well as convergence, with challenge as well as caution, with anticipation as well as acceptance.

There is no denying though that the middle aged often began to think in new ways about themselves, their families and the world in which they found themselves. There is no denying either that these changes sometimes seemed to occur rather abruptly and appeared to correspond remarkably closely to popular perceptions about what it was to be middle-aged.

The search for security

It is true, for example, that the middle aged tended to become increasingly concerned with security and stability. However, it was a concern that manifested itself in several ways, and ways that changed significantly during the course of the century. Although there was probably little change in the underlying financial concerns of those in their forties and fifties, there was a significant change in the ways that they thought about the physical aspects of the ageing process.

It was seen in Chapter 4 that the middle aged tended to be more concerned than young adults with attempting to secure a degree of long-term financial security. Of course, it is important to distinguish between circumstances and attitudes, between the ability and the desire to prepare for the future. The fact that the middle aged were more likely than those from younger age groups to seek financial security could be a reflection of their growing prosperity rather than of their growing anxiety.

In fact, there seems little doubt that the middle-aged concern for security and stability was a reflection both of growing prosperity and of growing anxiety. Those in their forties and fifties could scarcely fail to recognise that although they were probably better off than they had been when younger, their prosperity often rested upon alarmingly insecure foundations. Even the most optimistic projection of health, employment and family responsibilities was unlikely to reassure them that the existing balance between income and expenditure would be maintained in the long term.[4]

The financial anxieties of middle age seemed almost to transcend time, place, gender and class. In the 1920s and early 1930s, ex-RAF mechanic John Evans worked as a fitter, traveller, pedlar and salesman but was told 'time after time' while still in his thirties that he was too old to obtain the jobs that he wanted. He had a good idea what the future was likely to hold in store: 'some of my friends who are over 40 know for a fact that they'll never get another job while we live under this present system'.[5] In the early 1990s, celebrity columnist Mariella Frostrup recognised the signs of middle-aged anxiety while still in her very early thirties.

> I fear middle age really has struck. Hot on the heels of my valiant and continuing attempt to give up smoking comes the committing of nearly every penny I earn to a variety of pensions, insurance policies and life assurance.
>
> I now have a policy for all eventualities. One protects me if I'm unable to work . . . another guarantees a better salary on retirement than I could ever earn; a third will pay me a lump sum in 10 years; and then there's the one that pays my mother an even greater amount if I drop dead.[6]

Frostrup's reference to trying to give up smoking leads naturally to a consideration of the extent to which middle age brought about a shift in attitudes towards physical, as well as financial, well-being.[7] In fact, middle-aged attitudes towards physical health were a good deal more complicated than those towards financial security. The onset of middle age certainly tended to bring about a change in the ways that those in their forties and fifties regarded their physical well-being, but it was a change which itself changed significantly

4. J. Urquhart-Stewart, 'Life Begins at 40', *Independent Weekend*, 28 October 1995; Wolverhampton Oral History Project (hereafter WOH), Dr A., Mrs B., Mr C., Ms E.; *Ageing International*, Summer 1979.

5. J. Burnet, *Idle Hands: The Experience of Unemployment, 1790–1990*, Routledge, 1994, p. 218; *Daily Telegraph*, 23 August 1995.

6. *Sunday Times*, 11 December 1994, Also 'Cigarettes', *Mintel*, April 1974; *Daily Telegraph*, 23 August 1995; WOH, Mr N., Mrs Q.

7. The middle aged (and elderly) became concerned too about their safety, *Guardian*, 1 June 1994.

during the course of the century. Until the 1960s and 1970s those in their forties and fifties who were concerned about their health would probably try to take it easy; during the 1980s and 1990s they were much more likely to attempt to take some form of exercise – or at least to feel guilty if they failed to do so.

During the first half of the century, the middle aged were advised – and seemed to accept – that they should wrap up warm and be careful not to overdo it. The *Family Doctor* warned its readers in 1910 that the middle aged should avoid going out without an overcoat or engaging in the strenuous exercise that they had been able to undertake when younger. 'Youth will play tennis all the afternoon and evening; middle-age is quite content with one set.'[8] A Lancashire office worker wrote to a Sunday newspaper in the late 1940s about an alarming case in which a 'middle-aged man took up bowls and is now in hospital for an internal operation'.[9] Even thirty years later, a Wolverhampton primary school headmaster felt that once he was forty he would have to give up refereeing his pupils' football matches.[10]

Such caution became increasing unacceptable. During the second half of the century the middle aged, along with everybody else, were advised – and began to accept – that the best way to protect their health was by being active rather than inactive. The jogging boom of the 1970s and 1980s proved particularly attractive to those in their thirties and forties. As James Fixx argued in his 1977 best-seller *The Complete Book of Running*, when you're forty 'You'll actually start looking forward to your birthdays'.[11] Bruce Tulloh reinforced the message a few years later in his book *The Complete Distance Runner*,

> The encouraging thing about taking up running late in life is that for a while you can run the clock backwards. The average unfit thirty-five-year old would be doing well to run 6 miles in under 50 minutes, but five years later he could be running it under 35 minutes, and twenty years later he could still be in better physical condition than he had been at thirty-five.[12]

8. *Family Doctor*, 19 March 1910, Also 22 October 1910.
9. G. Snowdon to *Sunday Graphic*, 29 August 1948.
10. Information from Clare Benson.
11. J. F. Fixx, *The Complete Book of Running*, Penguin, 1981, p. 103.
12. B. Tulloh, *The Complete Distance Runner*, Panther, 1983, p. 216. Also M. Featherstone and M. Hepworth, 'Age and Inequality: Consumer Culture and the New Middle Age', in D. Robbins (ed.), *Rethinking Social Inequality*, Gower, Aldershot, 1982, pp. 110–11.

Such promises most certainly had an effect. The streets seemed to be full of joggers, many of them well into middle age. It was estimated in the mid-late 1970s that 15 per cent of all runners were over forty, and it was reported in 1985 that the most common age for men competing in the first four London marathons was 38.[13] Motives were mixed, but the desire to feel better and live longer was nearly always to the fore. A middle-aged jogger explained to *Jogging Magazine* in 1979 that running was more than just something to do. It gave him a 'general feeling of well-being and alertness, being taut and crisp'. 'Then of course, there is the slight smugness when you think, I'm better than the next man, I also feel that my chances of survival are better.'[14]

More striking still was the fact that even those who resisted the blandishments of the exercise enthusiasts very often believed that they were wrong to do so. In 1995, for example, *The Times* carried an article entitled 'How to recognise symptoms of the seriously middle-aged'. The first of the twenty tell-tale signs to watch out for cut straight to the heart of the matter.

> You start seeking out newspaper articles which suggest that jogging, squash and swimming are bad for you, and then quoting them to dangerously fit people at dinner parties. Ditto articles which show the French live for ever because they drink a bottle of claret a day.[15]

Censoriousness and conservatism

It seems to be accepted almost without question that it was usual for those in their forties and fifties to become increasingly censorious and conservative as they grew older.[16] Indeed, some of the assumptions made about middle-aged attitudes should cause even those least worried about age and ageing to pause and reflect. For as Barrie Stacey has pointed out, 'It is part of conventional political wisdom that people typically become more conservative as they grow older'.

> In this context the word 'conservative' has several meanings: cautious, unwilling to take risks, opposed to hasty changes or innovations, strongly supportive of the existing system of law and order, convinced

13. *Athletics Weekly,* 20 April 1985.
14. Featherstone and Hepworth, 'Age and Inequality', p. 109.
15. *The Times,* 18 March 1995.
16. See, for example, 'Reflections of Middle Age', *Punch,* 27 January 1909.

of the value of authority and obedience; resistance or active opposi-
tion to influences for general change in society or many specific kinds
of change or change which is viewed as a threat to the existing social
order, disposed to maintain existing institutions and traditions; belief
that human nature inevitably leads to inequality, conflict, aggression
and suffering; anti-egalitarian and resistant to change which would
benefit disadvantaged segments of the population.[17]

The censoriousness of the middle aged manifested itself, many
believed, in the moral judgements that they liked to make and
in the sexual inhibitions that they so often displayed. The middle
aged, it seemed, were more likely than other age groups to feel
themselves morally superior. How could young people carry on as
they did, worried generation upon generation of the middle aged.[18]
How could old people be so selfish and inward looking, they won-
dered. 'Have people of my age – round about 40 – different moral
standards to those aged 60 or more?', demanded a Leeds man in
1950. It was a question prompted by nothing more than the fact
that he had learned that the non-smoking, old-age pensioner wife
of a smoker intended to draw her tobacco allowance at a preferen-
tial rate and pass it on to her husband.[19]

The middle aged, it seemed, were more likely than other age
groups to be sexually repressed. The oral and autobiographical
sources that are available provide ample evidence of middle-aged
disapproval of anything remotely resembling sexual promiscuity.
Elizabeth Roberts concluded from her investigation of life in Barrow, Lancaster and Preston that 'Decades of Victorian attitudes had
produced, by the turn of the twentieth century, a generation of
working-class parents who were extremely prudish. Even when they
were very small, brothers and sisters were not allowed to see any
part of each other's naked bodies.'[20] The 1994 National Survey of
Sexual Attitudes and Lifestyles appeared to confirm the continuing
validity of such generalisation. It revealed, for instance, that the
middle aged were more likely than young adults to disapprove of
premarital sex, sex outside marriage and homosexual relationships
of any kind.[21]

17. B. Stacey, *Political Socialization in Western Society: An Analysis from a Life-span
Perspective*, Arnold, 1978, p. 138.
18. For example, *Daily Mail*, 7 May 1925, 8 January 1965; WOH, Dr A., Mr C.
19. R. Clarke to *Daily Sketch*, 1 September 1950.
20. E. Roberts, *A Woman's Place: An Oral History of Working-class Women*, Blackwell,
Oxford, 1984, p. 15.
21. K. Wellings, J. Field, A. M. Johnson and J. Wadsworth, *Sexual Behaviour in Britain:
The National Survey of Sexual Attitudes and Lifestyles*, Penguin, 1994, pp. 244–55.

In fact, even those activities that seemed on the face of it to offer evidence of middle-aged sexuality were often interpreted as providing indications of middle-aged repression. When middle-aged (and elderly) men looked at young women or read girlie magazines, it was seen as a sign less of sexual interest than of sexual incapacity – the inability of 'dirty old men' to find real-life women of their own. When middle-aged (and elderly) men took a sexual interest in children, it was regarded not only as a perversion but also as a sign of repression and of social and sexual immaturity.[22]

The conservatism of the middle aged manifested itself most strikingly, many people believed, in their political attitudes and voting behaviour. Barrie Stacey puts it with proper academic caution. 'It is often maintained that older persons are more likely than younger persons to hold conservative political views and to support right-wing political parties.'[23] There is a well-known aphorism that makes the point rather more bluntly: 'If you're not a radical at 20 you've no heart; if you're not a conservative at 60 you've no head.'[24]

It is a contention for which it is possible to marshall a good deal of empirical support. Interviews with those turning forty in the late 1950s and early 1960s suggest that it was not unusual for political views to shift to the right during middle age.[25] The introduction of public opinion polls in the 1960s makes available more systematic data about the relationship between age, attitudes and voting behaviour. Figures 6.1a, b and c are based upon a series of large-scale contemporary investigations, and seem to confirm the power and persistence of the association between middle age and Conservatism. Although the age categories selected are not ideal for the purposes of this book, they show that in the years following the Second World War there was a clear, and apparently causal, correlation between age and political allegiance. They reveal that in the six general elections held between 1945 and 1964, those in their fifties and early sixties were a great deal more likely to vote Conservative, and a great deal less likely to vote Labour, than those who were in their twenties. They reveal too that in the general elections of 1964 and 1987, those in their late thirties, forties and early fifties were

22. *Daily Sketch*, 23 January, 26 February 1970; University of Lancaster, Mrs H6B, p. 28. Men's magazines were aimed primarily at those aged under 35. *Mintel*, January 1977.

23. Stacey, *Socialization*, p. 138. Also J. Kingdom, *Government and Politics in Britain*, Polity Press, Cambridge, 1991, p. 171.

24. Cited in D. Denver, *Elections and Voting Behaviour in Britain*, Philip Allan, London, 1989, p. 33.

25. WOH, Mr J., Mr K.

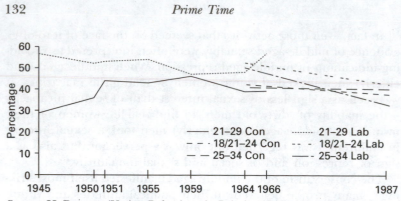

Sources: H. Durant, 'Voting Behaviour in Britain, 1945–66', in R. Rose (ed.), *Studies in British Politics: A Reader in Political Sociology*, Macmillan, 1969, p. 169; A. H. Halsey (ed.), *British Social Trends since 1900: A Guide to the Changing Social Structure of Britain*, Macmillan, 1988, p. 315.

Figure 6.1a   *Age and party allegiance, young adults, 1945–87*

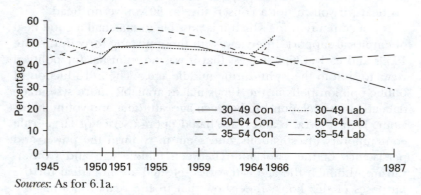

Sources: As for 6.1a.

Figure 6.1b   *Age and party allegiance, the middle aged, 1945–87*

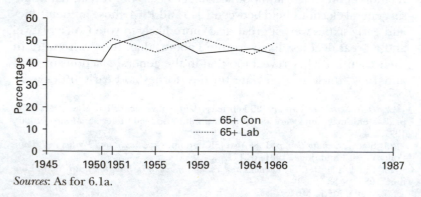

Sources: As for 6.1a.

Figure 6.1c   *Age and party allegiance, the elderly, 1945–66*

rather more likely to vote Conservative, and rather less likely to vote Labour, than those who were in their twenties and early thirties.

Nevertheless, there continues to be considerable debate as to the nature and cause of the correlation between age, political attitudes and voting behaviour. Some accept that age is the crucial factor, while others suggest that the major influence is generational, in particular the period in which one grows up and first begins to be influenced by political issues.[26] However, this is a debate that need not detain us here. For whatever the cause, there was – and is – a correlation between age and political allegiance. 'In terms of any general definition of conservatism, elderly people as a whole tend to be more conservative than middle-aged people and the latter to be more conservative than young adults.'[27]

The generation gap

It seems too that the middle aged believed that their interests were different from – and opposed to – those of other generations. It was when they reached their forties and fifties that many people began to think anew about the relationships between their own age group and those which came before and after them. Middle age, claimed Bernice Neugarten in 1967, was 'a period of heightened sensitivity to one's position within a complex social environment'.[28] The middle aged, it was agreed, tended to see themselves occupying a curious position, central yet contradictory.

> Generally the middle-ager sees himself as the bridge between the generations, both within the family and within the wider contexts of work and community. At the same time he has a clear sense of differentiation from both the younger and older generations.[29]

However, it was also agreed that the scale and significance of this so-called generation gap changed significantly during the course of the century. It was argued that until the 1960s or 1970s, the gap

26. Denver, *Elections*, pp. 33–4; D. Butler and D. Stokes, *Political Change in Britain: The Evolution of Electoral Choice*, St Martin's Press, 1974, pp. 48–66. Cf. N. D. Glenn and T. Hefner, 'Further Evidence on Aging and Party Identification', *Public Opinion Quarterly*, 36, 1972.

27. Stacey, *Socialization*, pp. 143–4.

28. B. L. Neugarten, 'The Awareness of Middle Age', in Owen (ed.), *Middle Age*, p. 55.

29. Neugarten, 'Awareness', p. 56.

between the middle aged and other age groups persisted and/or
grew wider. The Duke of Edinburgh claimed that by 1970, for
example, British society was split into age groups with no contact,
sympathy or understanding for one another.[30] It was suggested too
that this generation gap began to narrow from the 1970s onwards.
A *Times* columnist reported in 1995 that,

> Twenty years ago the generational strata kept to themselves. When
> I was 20 the only people I knew were 20 and neither 16-year-olds nor
> 25-year-olds came to my parties, nor I to theirs. But at the last party
> I threw there were a couple of 18-year-olds at one end of the range
> and a few 60-year-olds at the other, and neither seemed to think it
> odd that they or the others were there.[31]

This is to exaggerate. The middle aged always tended to find
young people difficult to deal with. They feared and resented the
freedom which they seemed to enjoy, and reacted with alarm both
to the apathy of the majority[32] and the 'symbolic provocation' of
the minority. Such challenge and reaction had a surprisingly long
history. 'Look at them well', exhorted the *Daily Graphic* at the turn
of the century.

> The boys affect a kind of uniform. No hat, collar, or tie is to be seen.
> All of them have a peculiar muffler twisted around the neck, a cap
> set rakishly forward, well over the eyes, and trousers very tight at the
> knee and very close to the foot. The most characteristic part of their
> uniform is the substantial leather belt heavily mounted with metal.
> It is not ornamental, but then it is not intended for ornament.[33]

Indeed, middle-aged anxiety almost certainly increased with the
invention – and re-invention – of the teenager. There were surges
of concern between the wars, in the late 1940s and again in the
early-mid 1960s.[34] 'I am not yet 40', explained a London man in

30. *Daily Sketch*, 13 January 1970, Also *Sunday Graphic*, 5 July 1931; University of
Lancaster, 'Family and Social Life in Barrow, Lancaster and Preston 1940–1970', Mr
59P, p. 20.

31. J. Diamond, 'Twenty Ways To Tell You're Middle-Aged', *The Times*, 18 March
1995. Also 'Act Your Age', Radio 4, 13 August 1995; M. Hepworth, 'The Mid Life Phase',
in G. Cohen (ed.), *Social Change and the Life Course*, Tavistock, 1987, pp. 142–3.

32. Leader in *Sunday Graphic*, 28 June 1931; John Higgs in Wolverhampton, *Express
and Star*, 4 August 1947.

33. G. Pearson, *Hooligan: A History of Respectable Fears*, Macmillan, Basingstoke,
1983, pp. 93–4. Also H. Travers, 'Growing Old Gracefully', *Wesleyan Methodist Magazine*, 149, 1926.

34. For example, D. Fowler, 'Teenage Consumers? Young Wage-earners and Leis-
ure in Manchester, 1919–1939', in A. Davies and S. Fielding (eds), *Workers' Worlds:
Cultures and Communities in Manchester and Salford, 1880–1939*, Manchester University
Press, Manchester, 1992.

1950, 'but when I see these oddities on the street corners I feel I belong to another world'.[35] As a Sussex University sociologist pointed out in the late 1960s, 'People who lived through the depession and the war are apt to feel that the young today are on a skive, having it good in a way they never did'.[36]

Such attitudes resulted, not surprisingly, in a good deal of resentment. In 1925, 'A Modern Girl' wrote to the *Daily Mail* to refute the suggestion that girls of her age were more degenerate than those of earlier generations.[37] Forty years later, a teenager from Buckinghamshire wrote to the same paper with virtually the same message.

> My hope in the coming year is that the older generation will cease to refer to the teenagers of today as a rude and ignorant rabble. Most young people are neither 'Mods' nor 'Rockers' nor any of the things associated with these names. As a teenager myself, I find that older people are just as rude and difficult to get on with as they think we are.[38]

In fact, the middle aged found it difficult to cope with even the most polite, helpful and conventional of young people. It was particularly galling to have to deal with those in their teens and twenties when they were in positions of any authority. A Staffordshire coalminer recalls the resentment he felt in the late 1940s when a twenty-five-year-old supervisor told him how to do a job which he had been doing for twenty years.[39] A stroke patient in her fifties explained in 1963 that she found it very hard to be given instructions by nurses no more than fifteen or sixteen years old.[40] The clichés were true: a middle-aged contributor to a radio programme on ageing confirmed in the mid 1990s that policemen really did seem to get younger as he grew older.[41]

Nor was this all. The middle aged also found it difficult to know how to deal with those who were older than themselves. Of course, relations between the middle aged and the elderly have never attracted anything like the attention devoted to the conflicts between the middle aged and those in their teens and early twenties. However, it seems that those in their forties and fifties reacted, once again, with a mixture of fear and resentment.

35. L. Hilton to *Sunday Graphic*, 6 August 1950.
36. M. Beloff, *The Plateglass Universities*, Secker and Warburg, 1968, p. 155.
37. *Daily Mail*, 7 May 1925.
38. *Daily Mail*, 8 January 1965. Also *Sunday Graphic*, 7 July 1935, 12 February 1950.
39. WOH, Mr J.   40. *Medical News*, 8 March 1963.   41. 'Act Your Age'.

Their fear is not difficult to understand. When the middle aged had dealings with the elderly, they saw only too clearly what might lie ahead of them. The middle aged, explained a doctor in 1957, commonly looked upon old age 'not as a challenge but as a threat'.[42] The middle aged, believes Betty Friedan, tend 'to exaggerate the expectation of dread decline after sixty-five'.

> The older one gets, the more frightened one is of being or becoming senile or showing other presumably age-related negative traits. . . . This fear is likely to motivate older people to distance themselves, psychologically, from older people with difficulties such as forgetfulness, by evaluating them as negatively as possible and thereby making them very different from themselves.[43]

The resentment of the middle aged is just as easy to understand. When those in their forties and fifties helped their ageing relatives or thought about the elderly population as a whole, they found it difficult to avoid seeing them as a burden, as a drain upon those who were economically active.[44] It was a resentment which peaked, not surprisingly, at times of economic difficulty and at times when the elderly population was believed to be growing faster than the population as a whole. In the late 1940s, the Royal Commission on Population predicted that the increasing number of older workers meant that 'the tendency will be for only the most exceptional of the younger people to be promoted. The prospects for the younger may become so poor that a powerful sense of frustration may arise.'[45] The 1980s and early 1990s witnessed an outpouring of middle-aged anxiety and resentment. When Mintel published its report *Does Life Begin at 50?* in 1995, it revealed that only 5 per cent of those aged 45–64 believed that they could look forward to an enjoyable and untroubled old age. The reason, they believed, lay in the economic and demographic squeeze in which they found themselves trapped. As Mintel's consumer research manager went on to explain,

> Just ten years ago, there were still dreams of early retirement for all, and the spending power to enjoy the new-found leisure time, but these have been thwarted because there are too few taxpayers to support increasing numbers of elderly people and by recession.[46]

42. Thomas Rudd in *Lancet*, 4 May 1957.
43. B. Friedan, *The Fountain of Age*, Vintage, 1994, pp. 24–5, 29.
44. A. Walker, 'The Age Gap and Wage Gap', *Guardian*, 18 September 1996.
45. *Royal Commission on Population, Report*, 1949, p. 120.
46. *The Times*, 23 August 1995.

Age and identity

It is scarcely surprising therefore that the middle aged grew more and more conscious of their age. Whatever their own experience of the ageing process and whatever the advice they were given on how to cope with it, they were increasingly given to understand that middle age had its own chronology and characteristics, its own problems and possibilities. The result was that those in their forties and fifties tended increasingly to be defined – and to define themselves – not just by their gender, region, religion, class and so on, but also by their age and generation.

The tendency of the middle aged to define themselves in this way manifested itself more and more often, in more and more ways. It was common from the very beginning of the century for those in their forties and fifties to comment wistfully on the passing of the years. In 1909, a contributor to *Punch* put his 'reflections of middle-age' to verse.

> Ah! how often you and I, my Gerald,
> Taking count of Time's appalling pace,
> Watching those insidious signs that herald
> Chronic apathy of form and face;
> Noting how our legs are not so lissome
> Nor our waists so waspish as of old,
> And the joys of youth how much we miss 'em,
> Vanished like the Age of Gold;[47]

The First World War reinforced the middle aged's sense of 'Time's appalling pace'. 'In the present crisis those who are middle-aged, although accustomed, perhaps, to regard themselves as in the "prime of life", have learnt to regret with sudden bitterness their lost youth.'[48] During the 1930s, a popular newspaper columnist explained that, 'Life Begins at 40' was 'A slogan gaily proclaimed by folk past the meridian, partly because they believe it and partly to knock the twenty-thirties who imagine they have all the fun'.[49] Indeed, by the end of the century, those entering their forties and fifties believed not only that they were middle-aged, but that their middle age was unlike any which had gone before. 'One day in the blessedly not-too-distant future', predicted an American commentator in 1996, 'the single greatest event in modern history will occur'.

47. *Punch*, 27 January 1909.   48. 'Active 54' to *Lancet*, 5 September 1914.
49. Sir J. Fraser in *Sunday Graphic*, 7 July 1935.

The baby boom generation will go boom. Finally, we will die off, and there will be a great cosmic sigh of relief.

The generation that has noisily demanded to be the centre of attention since conception will work its way through the valley of the shadow.[50]

It was but a short step from regret to denial. As was seen in Chapter 2, it became increasingly common to claim that age was less important than attitude, that one was only as old as one felt. It appears in fact that the more those in their forties and fifties were defined by their age, the more some of them fought against it. 'Today's society makes middle age an issue', observed a sixty-year-old magistrate in the mid 1990s, but 'As I've gone through life I didn't consider it'.[51]

It was a short step too from regret and denial to reassessment. It was essential, many felt as they reached middle age, to decide what was really important to them. It was the fortieth and fiftieth birthdays that seemed, not surprisingly, to act as the catalyst. As the heroine of Angus Wilson's *The Middle Age of Mrs Eliot* observed, 'keeping a lifeline to her youth had somehow become very important since she had turned forty'.[52] As Michael Caine remarked in his autobiography, he and his wife thought more and more about their priorities after he turned fifty. They

> decided that life was a lease, not a freehold, and as the years dwindled down, it became less valuable but more precious. We were going to cut out all the dross, we agreed. We were only going to go where we really wanted to go, and be with the people whom we really liked and loved. After the age of fifty, you become aware that your stay here is not permanent.[53]

Regret, denial and reassessment were associated with, and derived from, a growing awareness of death. It 'is this fact of the entry upon the psychological scene of the reality and inevitability of one's own eventual personal death', it was claimed, 'that is the central and crucial feature of the mid-life phase'.[54] 'Older people', it was believed, 'have always been more religious than the young.'[55] Not many were

50. *Guardian*, 9 July 1996.
51. WOH, Mrs O. Also Mrs B.; *Daily Mail*, 4 May 1935; Paul McCartney in *Chic*, January 1991.
52. A. Wilson, *The Middle Age of Mrs Eliot*, Secker and Warburg, 1958, p. 50.
53. M. Caine, *What's It All About?*, Arrow Books, 1992, p. 432.
54. E. Jacques, 'Death and the Mid-life Crisis', *International Journal of Psychoanalysis*, 46, October 1965, p. 506.
55. G. Davie, *Religion in Britain since 1945: Believing Without Belonging*, Blackwell, Oxford, 1994, pp. 117–21.

immune. 'I always used to think that I'd be dead by the time I was forty-five, and that thought didn't bother me', explained Francis Rossi of Status Quo in 1993.

> But now my ambition in life is to get old. I didn't think forty was going to be as good as it was and growing older has just kept getting better. . . . I used to see those old boys playing bowls and think 'You must be joking.' Now I think 'Oh, that looks nice.'[56]

The difficulty is to find the evidence that will allow the broader applicability of such claims to be tested empirically, that will make it possible to examine the attitudes of large groups of the middle aged at different periods of the century. The evidence is as scattered as one would expect. In 1942, Mass-Observation produced a *Report on Death and the Supernatural* which was based upon a two-year investigation using a hundred voluntary observers (half men and half women, half under forty and half over forty). It suggested that the relationship between age and death was a good deal more complicated than one might imagine. Those over forty were much more likely than those under forty to think about death, but much less likely to be afraid of it; those over forty were slightly more likely to be afraid of the process of dying, and were also slightly less likely to believe in an afterlife.[57]

In 1995, a radio programme on middle age confirmed, at least anecdotally, the continuing relevance of some of Mass-Observation's findings from fifty years before. Several speakers agreed that forty had marked a crucial turning point in their attitudes towards death. Before they were forty, they explained, they had believed in their own immortality and had been afraid, not of death, but of dying before they were able to do the things which they wanted. After they reached forty, their friends and parents began to die, and they became only too aware that what they had once regarded as their future was now quite definitely their present.[58]

Such complications and ambiguities can be seen too in attitudes towards making a will. Although the middle aged increasingly recognised the importance of making arrangements for their descendants, they remained extremely reluctant to take the action which they knew that they ought to. Even in the 1980s, acceptance and

56. F. Rossi and R. Parfitt, *Just for the Record: The Autobiography of Status Quo*, Bantam Press, 1993, p. 184. Also WOH, Dr A., Mrs E.; N. Gerrard, 'Melvyn's Dark Ages', *Observer*, 24 March 1996.
57. Mass-Observation, 1315, *Report on Death and the Supernatural*, 1942; 'The Unknown', *M-O Bulletin*, June 1942.
58. 'Act Your Age'.

denial remained inextricably entwined. A personnel officer from Lancaster admitted that although he urged his workers to make a will, he himself had never done so.[59] A stock controller from nearby Barrow-in-Furness explained why it was that even in her fifties she could not bring herself to sort out her affairs.

> I think it's the thought of what it is really that puts you off. Because sometimes John [her husband] say[s] you know, really we should make a will. And I say oh I don't want to though. It's just getting down to it really, it's the thought and actually doing it.[60]

It is clear then that popular views about the attitudes of the middle aged had a substantial basis in reality. There seems little doubt that when they reached their forties and fifties, many did begin to become more anxious, more cautious, more conservative and more conscious of their age. These were common, unsettling and easily derided changes, and their importance should be neither overlooked nor underestimated.

However, this is by no means the end of the matter. As was pointed out at the beginning of the chapter, it would be unwise to imagine that everybody in their forties and fifties was likely to react in the same way to the onset of middle age. Sometimes, it has been seen, the middle aged reacted in most unmiddle-aged ways, becoming more tolerant, moving to the left politically, and hankering not after stability and security but after change, uncertainty and excitement. In 1961, for instance, broadcaster Phil Drabble went to live in the country in order to open a nature reserve and try to forge a new career from writing: 'at the age of forty seven, I burned my boats . . . knowing only too well that if my work ran dry, my chances of retrieving a similar status in industry were pretty slim'. It was, he remembers, 'a gut churning time'.[61]

Indeed, it is possible to point to any number of factors that need to be taken into account when seeking to understand the reasons that the middle aged reacted in the ways that they did: everything from ethnic background and religious beliefs to marital status and sexual orientation. Nonetheless, it has been decided that in this chapter, as in those which have gone before, attention will be directed towards the most obvious, and it is believed the most important, determinants of middle-aged behaviour and belief: gender and class. It will be argued that women tended to react very differently

59. Lancaster, Mrs G3L, p. 79. Also Mrs M12B, pp. 74–5.
60. Lancaster, Mrs M12B, p. 75.
61. Drabble, *Voice*, pp. 88–9. Also WOH, Ms E., Mr F., Mr L.

from men, and that the middle class tended to react rather differently from the working class, to the onset of middle age. It will be
suggested, in other words, that gender and class cut across the easy
generalisations that are often made about the relationship between
age and attitudes.

Gender and generation

Women certainly did not react in the same way as men. It has been
seen that although the sharp distinctions that late nineteenth- and
early twentieth-century commentators had drawn between men's
and women's experience of ageing began to diminish, middle-aged
women continued to be stigmatised in many, if not most, aspects of
their lives. It has been seen too that such stigmatisation coincided
with, and reinforced, the other disadvantages that women suffered
when they reached their forties and fifties. The differences between
men's and women's health, standards of living and experiences of
family life all tended to grow wider in middle age. One does not
need to be wedded to the notion that ideas are materially determined to believe that middle-aged women were unlikely to look at
the world in the same way as middle-aged men.

It is true that middle-aged women became as worried as middle-
aged men about the need for security and stability. However, it was
a concern which, as might be expected, tended to manifest itself in
rather different ways. Yet these differences are easily missed if the
effort is not made to distinguish firmly between attitude and behaviour, between the desire and the ability to prepare for the future.
So while there is no reason to think that women were less keen than
men to secure a degree of long-term financial security, there is
every reason to suppose that they found it more difficult to do so.

It is probable therefore that whereas middle-aged men sought to
prepare for the future by holding on to their jobs and building up
what savings they could, women did so too by maintaining, and
seeking to strengthen, the family, kinship and neighbourhood ties
by which they were surrounded. It was seen in the previous chapter that the responsibility of caring for elderly relatives remained
more common and more powerful than is often supposed. Although
middle-aged women's relationships with the generation before them
were fundamentally non-exploitative, they were marked by a reci-
procity which did not necessarily exclude elements of calculation.[62]

62. For example, Benson, *Working Class*, ch. 5.

Indeed, it seems probable that anxiety about the future intensified during the 1980s and 1990s. The onset of economic depression,
the growth of female employment and the undermining of the welfare state meant that the policy of strengthening family, kinship and
neighbourhood ties placed formidable burdens upon those trying
to put them into practice. When Mintel published its 1995 report
Does Life Begin at 50?, the firm's consumer research manager concluded that, 'With more jobs being created for women than men,
those women over 40 and under 65 are not getting to put their
feet up and relax that they might have expected upon reaching
this age, whereas the men most certainly are'.[63]

Women and men also reacted differently to the physical changes
of middle age. It is well known, of course, that women of all ages
took less care than men to eat sensibly and to engage in regular
exercise.[64] It is scarcely surprising therefore that during the first
half of the century, middle-aged women were probably more ready
than middle-aged men to accept the advice which was given them
to take it easy when they reached their forties and fifties.[65]

Indeed, the differences in the way that women and men reacted
to middle age almost certainly grew more pronounced during the
second half of the century. Women proved a great deal slower than
men to follow the promptings of those urging the need to adopt a
more healthy diet and take more regular exercise. They knew that
they should change, but found it exceptionally difficult to do so.
Even members of the medical profession were often at a loss. A
fifty-year-old nurse told *Woman's Own* in 1994 that,

> When I hit 50, I thought I should start exercising – but that's as far
> as I got! Any attempt to watch my diet just makes me miserable, so
> I think I'll wait until I'm 60 and then take up something gentle, like
> swimming.[66]

The evidence is not solely anecdotal. A survey conducted in 1990
revealed that women in their fifties were slightly more likely than
men of the same age to smoke,[67] and an investigation carried out

63. *The Times*, 23 August 1995. Also *Guardian*, 23 August 1995.
64. See H. Jones, *Health and Society in Twentieth-century Britain*, Longman, 1994,
pp. 182–5; Neugarten, 'Awareness', p. 61.
65. R. Hoggart, *The Uses of Literacy: Aspects of Working-class Life with Special Reference
to Publications and Entertainments*, Pelican, 1958, pp. 41, 46.
66. *Woman's Own*, 21 February 1994.
67. However, they were unlikely to smoke as heavily. Carnegie Inquiry into the
Third Age, *Health: Abilities and Wellbeing in the Third Age*, Carnegie Trust, 1992,
pp. 76–8.

five years later confirmed that middle-aged women generally did less than middle-aged men to look after their health.

> Women over 45 are more stressed than men. Far more women than men smoke, far fewer take exercise, and a fifth over 45 and under 54 said they were often in too much of a rush to eat a proper meal.[68]

It was not simply that they knew what they should be doing, but were unable to do it. In some respects women's attitudes towards their health were the reverse of men's. Whereas men tended to feel guilty when they did not try to live more healthily, women seemed to feel guilty when they did. A forty-seven-year-old secretary explained in the mid 1990s how hard she was trying to fend off middle age – but then denied that she was doing so.

> About three years ago I decided to start eating more healthily, so the whole family went on a wholefood diet with skimmed milk and less sugar. I go to the gym three times a week to keep myself in trim but I certainly don't worry about ageing. I am the way I am and nothing's really going to change that.[69]

Middle-aged women were also depicted as still more frustrated, censorious and conservative than their male counterparts. The changes associated with the menopause, explained a medical expert in 1930, were ideological as well as physical: they 'are permanent, and are the hallmarks of middle age. Such are wrinkles, grey hair, and a calmer, if more conservative and less romantic, outlook on life'.[70] Other commentators maintained that although women became more romantically inclined in middle age, they were able to express their feelings only indirectly.

> Middle-aged women, we are led to believe, have no sexuality, only a longing for vicarious romance, which is consumed through the pages of Mills and Boon or what Hollywood used to call the 'woman's picture' – *Pretty Woman*, or *When Harry Met Sally*, or *Sleepless in Seattle*.[71]

Of course, it is not at all easy to compare the censoriousness of middle-aged men and women. It depends not only upon how censoriousness is defined and measured, but also upon who it is that is doing the defining and measuring. The popular press was increasingly keen to uncover examples of middle-aged women's sexual voracity. The *Daily Sketch* reported in 1959 that a Liverpool holiday

---

68. *The Times*, 23 August 1995. Also *Guardian*, 23 August 1995.
69. *Woman's Own*, 21 February 1994.
70. George Riddoch in *British Medical Journal*, 13 December 1930.
71. L. Grant, 'Single Woman, Fortysomething, Seeks Companionship and Sex . . .', *Guardian*, 6 February 1994.

club was concerned to 'stop any more middle-aged spinsters chasing and embarrassing youths on holidays abroad'. The solution adopted, the paper explained with some glee, was to ask women holiday-makers their age – and then to add on another ten years.[72] The serious press was not above such titillation. In 1994, the *Guardian* carried a lengthy feature entitled, 'Single Woman, Fortysomething, Seeks Companionship and Sex . . .', in which five middle-class, middle-aged women talked 'candidly about their prospects of love and sexual fulfilment'.

> 'I've found that sex in my forties has been the best sex ever,' Sally argues. 'Much better than sex in my twenties and thirties. The quality of lovemaking, I couldn't compare it. My marriage was dreadful and my promiscuous stage was awful. I didn't learn anything until I was in my forties.[73]

However, middle-aged women's attitudes in sexual matters usually remained a good deal more prosaic and conventional than the *Guardian*'s sensationalism would lead one to suppose, When Social and Community Planning Research investigated attitudes towards sexual permissiveness during the 1980s, it discovered that 35–54-year-old women were more likely than younger women and men of the same age to wish to see pornographic films and magazines banned, and less likely than members of these other age groups to approve of young people being given contraceptive advice and supplies without their parents being informed.[74]

It is not surprising therefore that middle-aged women were invariably depicted as conservative in their political attitudes, affiliations and voting behaviour. Although psephologists and political scientists have paid remarkably little attention to the relationship between age, gender and politics, the work which they have done on age and politics and on gender and politics suggests that middle-aged women were more conservative than many other groups in society. David Denver concludes, for example, that in the 1950s and 1960s, 'younger people . . . were more inclined to vote Labour while older voters favoured the Conservatives', and 'men were less likely to vote Conservative and more likely to vote Labour than women'.[75]

---

72. *Daily Sketch*, 9 January 1959. Also *Sunday Graphic*, 3 May 1931; *News of the World*, 1 October 1995; *Sunday Mirror*, 25 February 1996; G. Greer, *The Change: Women, Ageing and the Menopause*, Penguin, 1992, p. 324.

73. *Guardian*, 6 February 1994. Also Greer, *Change*, p. 321ff.

74. Social & Community Planning Research, *British Social Attitudes: The Fifth Report*, Gower, Aldershot, 1989, pp. 37–8, 40, 47. Also WOH, Mrs B.

75. Denver, *Elections*, pp. 33–4. Also V. Randall, *Women and Politics: An International Perspective*, Macmillan, Basingstoke, 1987, p. 69.

Fortunately, it is possible to use the evidence available from public opinion polls to submit the supposed correlation between age, gender and political affiliation to slightly more sustained scrutiny than it normally receives. When this is done, it becomes clear that the relationship is considerably more complicated than some views allow. It was found that in 1964 for example, 'generational differences among women were pronounced':

> while older women voted Conservative at about the same rate as men of their age, and while middle-aged (30 to 59) women were 8 percentage points ahead of men in their rate of Conservative voting, young women voted Labour at a rate (57 per cent) 11 points higher than young men.[76]

However, it is unclear, once again, whether these differences were the result simply of the interaction between gender and the life cycle. It may be, it has been pointed out, that generation was as important as age, that 'older women's conservatism' was the 'result of their assimilation of partisan values at a time when the Labour Party was not yet perceived as a viable contender for national power'.[77] In all events, it seems that from the 1960s onwards the association between age, gender and Conservatism began to weaken as educational opportunities widened, and religious and other traditional values became less widely accepted.[78]

Middle-aged women also thought differently from middle-aged men about the generations that came before and after them. This is another daunting issue to discuss historically, yet what emerges is not an altogether surprising contradiction. It seems that although women's ageing was stigmatised much more than men's, women were possibly less frightened and resentful than men when dealing with teenagers and young adults. It seems too that because women took on the burden of caring for elderly relatives, they were probably more frightened and resentful than their husbands and partners when confronted by members of their parents' generation.[79]

76. Randall, *Women and Politics*, p. 71.
77. Randall, *Women and Politics*, p. 71. Also J. G. Francis and G. Peele, 'Reflections on Generational Analysis: Is There a Shared Political Perspective Between Men and Women?', *Political Studies*, 26, 1978; J. Evans, 'Women and Politics: A Re-appraisal', *Political Studies*, 28, 1980, pp. 215–16.
78. Information from Julie Skucha, a postgraduate student at the University of Wolverhampton.
79. *Daily Telegraph*, 23 August 1995.

It is clear, of course, that middle-aged women, like middle-aged men, became more conscious of their age as they grew older. Women, like men, were given to understand that middle age brought its own problems and possibilities; and women, like men, tended increasingly to be defined – and to define themselves – by their age as well as by their gender, region, religion and class. However, when women thought about the ageing process, they did not do so in the same way as men. Women, it seems, were less likely to regret the passing of the years, less likely to deny the importance of age, and more likely to use middle age as an opportunity for the reassessment and reordering of their priorities.

The first of these claims will come as a surprise. It would seem on the face of it that women were a great deal more likely than men to regret the passing of the years. As has been seen already, it seemed to be accepted as almost axiomatic that for women biology and destiny were inextricably entwined. It was commonly believed that the coming of the menopause meant that a woman's best years were behind her, and that this was why middle-aged women became so obsessed with the loss of their looks. *Woman's Own* explained towards the beginning of the century that, 'Youth is, to a woman, one of her most treasured possessions, yet she does not know it is a treasure until it has dropped from her heedless grasp'.[80] The editor of *Woman's Journal* admitted eighty years later that, 'The real horror of being 40 and female is that you know full well that your chances of being called a sex kitten again are slim. Building sites remain eerily silent as you swing past.'[81]

Single women and those who were separated and divorced were supposed to find the passing of the years particularly difficult to cope with, Certainly, the problem pages of women's magazines carried a stream of letters from single women in their forties and fifties. There's 'nothing for the unmarried, middle-aged woman', complained one of Evelyn Home's readers in 1958. 'We're the forgotten army'.[82] They continued to feel excluded. 'Kindly platitudes won't solve *my* problem', protested one of Home's correspondents in the early 1970s. 'I'm forty, single, a virgin – one of thousands.'[83]

In fact, women's attitudes towards the ageing process were a good deal more complicated than such views suggest. There are two major factors that need to be taken into account. It should be

---

80. *Woman's Own*, 3 July 1915. Also Friedan, *Fountain of Age*, p. 113.
81. *Express and Star*, 1995. Also *Sunday Graphic*, 26 April 1931, 7 July 1935; *Daily Mail*, 4 May 1935.
82. *Woman*, 8 November 1958.
83. *Woman*, 17 January 1970. Also *News of the World*, 15 October 1995.

remembered first that women were often pleasantly surprised to discover that the menopause proved less traumatic than they had been led to believe. They knew far better than any doctor that, 'The life expectancy of a woman greatly exceeds that of her repro- ductive organs'.[84] It should be recognised too that women were possibly better than men at dealing with the dislocation and uncer- tainty of middle age. Could it be, asks Betty Friedan, that 'the very discontinuity and change that has taken place in women's roles over a lifetime – *their continual practice in retirement and disengagement, shift and reengagement* – account for their greater flexibility and resilience in age?'[85]

In so far as generalisation is possible, it seems that middle-aged women were probably less likely than middle-aged men to deny the importance of age, and more likely to see their forties and fifties as an opportunity to reassess and reorder their priorities. However, the evidence, it must be conceded, is scattered and slight, the argu- ment speculative rather than conclusive.

There are some indications that women were less prone than men to denying the importance of age. As they grew older, women became more inclined to agree that comfort was of greater import- ance than fashion.[86] As they reached middle age, they became con- cerned not to dress in ways which were perceived as inappropriate. A forty-two-year-old woman from Bournemouth put her thoughts to verse in 1970.

> Growing old gracefully
> Is terribly hard to do.
> You *feel* you're only twenty-one,
> But *know* you're forty-two.
> You shorten skirts an inch or so,
> And take to the bottle of bleach.
> But you end up looking a bit of a prune
> Instead of a blooming peach.[87]

A quarter of a century later, fifty-three-year-old Esmee Nicholls was living in nearby Weymouth with her husband Roger. 'I buy clothes that Roger likes, as I trust his judgement. I go for suits in one

---

84. *Lancet*, 7 June 1975. Also 23 October 1943, 17 July 1982, *British Medical Journal*, 15 May 1976.
85. Friedan, *Fountain of Age*, p. 112. Also M. Bernard, C. Itzin, C. Phillipson and J. Skucha, 'Gendered Work, Gendered Retirement', in S. Arber and J. Ginn (eds), *Connecting Gender and Ageing: A Sociological Approach*, Open University Press, Bucking- ham, 1995, p. 57.
86. 'Women's Shoes', *Mintel*, July 1975, pp. 33–40.
87. Mrs E. T. to *Woman*, 10 January 1970.

colour, and plain or printed dresses, but nothing too fashionable as I don't want to look like mutton dressed as lamb.'[88] Such caution was not surprising given the vitriolic attacks suffered by celebrities who tried too hard to stem the passing of the years. 'Dear Fay Weldon', wrote one journalist in 1995, 'I was horrified by your confession – actually, it was more like a schoolgirl manifesto – published in the *Mail on Sunday* that not only have you had an expensive face-lift, but you're also tempted by liposuction . . .

> Fay, have you gone stark, raving mad? . . .
> Frankly, Fay, you sound as though you've entered the cocoon (and I use this word advisedly) of age crisis. Instead of accepting mortality sensually, poetically, philosophically, you have gone into a panic-driven spiral of denial. I need to tell you that facelifts are not the answer.[89]

There are some indications too that, especially towards the end of the century, women were more likely than men to see middle age as an opportunity to decide afresh what they wanted to do with the rest of their lives. They were most certainly urged to think in this way. 'Once the empty nest is recognised as a major rite of passage and the feelings acknowledged and worked through, the horizons are limitless', they were told in 1995. 'It is at this stage that we can truly have it all.'[90]

This was mere hyperbole. But there is some evidence that the middle aged did begin to recognise and welcome the opportunity for reassessment that middle age brought with it. Those who can remember the early years of the century see clearly that in this respect, as so many others, attitudes have changed significantly. The seventy-nine-year-old wife of a Staffordshire builder recalls that, 'My grandparents were middle-aged before we were. The ladies were very old fashioned and were more at home and they didn't lead the life that we did when we became middle-aged' in the late 1950s. 'We were freer and more active. They accepted it more than we did.'[91] Some were still more enthusiastic. 'Being made redund-ant at the age of 45 was the best thing that could have happened to me', claimed Cynthia Nock from Birmingham in 1996.

> Friends and colleagues often asked me where I bought my clothes and how I managed to be so organised while keeping fit and looking

88. *Woman's Own*, 14 August 1995. Also 21 February 1994.
89. *Independent*, 5 September 1995. Also *Guardian*, 16 June 1994.
90. S. Bovey, 'Home Alone – For Mothers', *Guardian*, 8 September 1995. Also Win, 'One Little Chat Changed My Life', *Woman's Own*, 11 September 1995.
91. WOH, Mrs I.

good. . . . So I decided to set up a lifestyle consultancy to help them. . . . Not only do I help others but they help me, too, as we have a laugh and a chat. I've just turned 50 and I feel great. Anyone who thinks life gets dull as middle age approaches, forget it.[92]

Class, caution and contradiction

The middle class and working class reacted no more uniformly than men and women to the onset of middle age. Although the clear distinction that earlier generations had drawn between middle-class and working-class ageing began to be applied less confidently, it continued to be accepted that working people aged earlier, and less satisfactorily, than those from managerial and professional backgrounds. Such views reflected, and no doubt reinforced, the very real material, psychological and emotional differences that separated the classes. For as was seen in earlier chapters of the book, class differences in health and health care persisted into middle age, while differences in material conditions tended, if anything, to grow wider still as people entered their forties and fifties.

Nevertheless, the relationship between age, class and attitudes is no easier to disentangle than that between age, gender and attitudes. The evidence is scattered, generalisation is difficult, and it is important to stress, yet again, that the arguments which are put forward in this part of the book should be treated less as conclusions to be accepted than as propositions to be tested.

It does seem, however, that the middle aged, both middle-class and working-class, worried about the need for security and stability. Yet this was a concern which, as might be expected, tended to manifest itself in different ways – and ways which once again are easily missed if the effort is not made to distinguish between the desire and the ability to prepare for the future. So while middle-aged workers, like middle-aged managers and professionals, were no doubt keen to secure a degree of long-term financial security, they knew how difficult it would be for them to do so. It is possible therefore that working people, like women, sought not only to protect their jobs and put by some savings, but also to maintain and strengthen the family, kinship and neighbourhood ties from which they might hope to derive some benefit in the future.[93]

92. Reference mislaid. Also anonymous letter to *Woman's Journal*, December 1994; *Daily Mail*, 4 May 1996; A. Davis-Goff, *Walled Gardens: Scenes from an Anglo-Irish Childhood*, Picador, 1990, p. 237.
93. F. Zweig, *The British Worker*, Penguin, 1952, pp. 57–8.

It seems too that the middle class and working class reacted differently to the physical changes of middle age. It is well known that working people of all ages were less concerned – and less able – than those from other classes to protect themselves against threats to their health.[94] It is not surprising therefore that middle-aged workers proved much slower than middle-aged managers and professionals to follow the advice which they were given to eat sensibly, to exercise regularly and to think positively. It was found in the mid 1970s, for example, that the heaviest of all smokers were middle-aged, working-class men, the proportion of smokers in social groups A and B standing at 14–15 per cent, while the proportion to be found in groups D and E averaged around 25–26 per cent.[95]

Evidence of the relationship between age, class and morality is somewhat more elusive. It was often assumed that the working class were less tolerant than the middle class, and the middle aged less open-minded than young adults. It is not easy to substantiate even such relatively straightforward claims – and it is a great deal more difficult to uncover the evidence required to permit more complicated comparisons to be made. However, investigations carried out during the 1980s permit some limited progress to be achieved. When Social and Community Planning Research questioned a national sample of respondents about their attitudes towards pornography in 1983 and 1987, it confirmed that the middle aged were less critical than the elderly, and the middle class less censorious than the working class. Those from middle-class backgrounds were less keen to ban pornographic films and magazines, and were more prepared to allow doctors to supply young people with family planning advice and contraceptive supplies without informing their parents.[96] It seems reasonable to conclude therefore that in this period at least the commonly held consensus about the correlation between age, class and moral attitudes was based upon tolerably secure empirical foundations.

The relationship between age and political attitudes, and between class and political attitudes has attracted a great deal of attention – but that between age, class and political attitudes almost none at all.[97] So although it has been seen that the middle aged were more likely than young adults to sympathise with the Conservatives, and it can be shown that the middle class were more sympathetic to Conservatism than the working class, it remains irritatingly difficult to isolate the age and class foundations of middle-aged political

94. Jones, *Health*, pp. 172–8.   95. 'Cigarettes', *Mintel*, April 1974; March 1977.
96. *British Social Attitudes*, 5th Report, p. 47. Also WOH, Mrs P.
97. See, for example, Denver, *Elections*, p. 138.

attitudes and voting behaviour. Two leading commentators concluded in the mid 1980s that,

> The electoral effect of age is virtually nil. In 1983 the Conservatives were in the lead among all age groups. . . . When the electorate is divided at age 45, the Standardized Index of Determination is very low, 2 per cent.
>
> When controls are introduced for class, a limited difference in party preferences emerges. . . . The effect of age, after controlling for class, is on average 12 per cent for Conservatives, 6 per cent for Labour, and 5 per cent for the Alliance.[98]

It is impossible, of course, to quantify class differences in the ways that the middle aged regarded the generations that preceded and followed them. Yet class differences there were, with those from the middle class particularly fearful and critical of young people. Geoffrey Pearson has demonstrated convincingly the power and persistence of the 'respectable fears' that arose when the middle class were confronted by working-class youth.[99] Indeed, there is evidence that such fears – or something very like them – were aroused too by the sight of middle-class teenagers and young adults. There is the tendency to be 'snobbish in a small-time way', reported John Diamond in 1995. He recognised, he believed,

> the almost middle-aged middle classes having an indulgent laugh at the aimless, youthful middle-classes who don't have the social or financial wherewithal to strive for anything better than a pint and a slippery dance on a Saturday night.[100]

There was one further way in which the classes differed in their reactions to the onset of middle age. The middle aged, whether middle-class or working-class, grew increasingly conscious of their age, but they tended to draw rather different conclusions about what it was which they and those about them were experiencing. The middle class, it seems, were more likely than the working class to regret the passing of the years, and more likely, by the end of the century, to use middle age as an opportunity for reassessment and re-evaluation.

Unfortunately, this is a dichotomy that it is easier to illustrate than it is to substantiate. Indeed, it is possible to be seduced by the superior literacy and practised articulacy of the middle class into identifying class differences where none existed. Nonetheless, it

98. R. Rose and I. McAllister, *Voters Begin to Choose: From Closed-class to Open Elections in Britain*, Sage, 1986, p. 67.
99. G. Pearson, *Hooligan: A History of Respectable Fears*, Macmillan, Basingstoke, 1983.
100. *The Times Magazine*, 17 June 1995.

does seem that those from the middle class found it more difficult than those from the working class to accept the passing of the years. Setting more store perhaps by such 'youthful' qualities as energy, enterprise and success, they coped less well with the physical, psychological and material changes which they, and others, regarded as typical of the middle years.[101] It has been suggested, for example, that the poor accepted middle age more easily than the better off because it offered married couples a brief period of relative prosperity,[102] and promised wives relief from what were regarded as the unwelcome sexual demands of their husbands.[103]

It seems too that those from the middle class were more likely than those from the working class to use middle age as an opportunity for reassessment and re-evaluation. It was seen in the previous chapter that it was middle-class women who were most likely to develop new, and higher, expectations of marriage when they reached their forties and fifties. This was part of a broader divergence. Middle-class women often focused upon the new possibilities which they saw opening up before them, whereas working-class women tended to remain wedded to the view that the responsibilities of early adulthood would be followed all too soon by the deterioration of middle age. It was found tellingly, if not surprisingly, that towards the end of the century members of social classes A and B were more than twice as likely than those from classes D and E to decide to return to academic study.[104]

It is clear then that the relationship between age and attitudes was less secure than is usually believed. So while it is true that the biological, material and other developments of middle age were associated with changes in the way that those in their forties and fifties looked at the world, it is not at all easy to generalise about the direction, scale and importance of these changes. The middle aged were no more likely than any other age group to think in identical ways about the world in which they found themselves. To suggest otherwise would be to perpetuate a caricature in a way that constitutes almost wilful misrepresentation.

101. *Punch*, 2 February 1910; *Sunday Graphic*, 7 July 1935; *Daily Mail*, 2 May 1955; *British Medical Journal*, 18 November 1967; P. Beaumont, 'Thirtysomethings Who Won't Grow Up', *Observer*, 19 May 1996.
102. Arthur Calder-Marshall cited in M. Featherstone and M. Hepworth, *Surviving Middle Age*, Blackwell, Oxford, 1982, p. 56.
103. A. P. Thompson cited in *Lancet*, 28 March 1936; 23 October 1943.
104. Carnegie Inquiry into the Third Age, *Learning: Education, Training and Information in the Third Age*, Carnegie Trust, 1992, p. 13.

CHAPTER SEVEN

Conclusion

It is never easy to assess the importance of one's own research. It is possible therefore that the writing of this book has been little more than a form of therapy, a way for a middle-aged author to try to cope with some of the difficulties of the ageing process.[1] It is possible too that the writing of this book has been of less value academically than this conclusion will suggest. It is always tempting for authors to exaggerate the significance of their work, to suggest in this case that it makes a contribution which will modify – and perhaps transform – our understanding not just of age and ageing but also of the way in which British society has developed during the past hundred years or so.

Such temptations must be avoided as best one can. Nonetheless, it is believed that the arguments put forward in this book are of considerable originality and importance. Indeed, given historians' failure to confront directly the experience of the middle aged, it is not too far-fetched to suggest that this – or almost any – study of the subject must constitute a reasonably significant advance in our understanding of a fundamental but easily overlooked aspect of modern British economic, social and cultural history.

Three broad propositions have been advanced. It has been shown that there developed a growing disjuncture between the representation and the reality of middle-aged life. On the one hand, it came to be accepted that middle age was a period of decline and convergence: these were the years, it was believed, during which the differences of early adulthood gave way, in the face of decay and decline, to the dispiriting homogeneity of early and late middle age. On the other hand, it has been shown that such views are

1. B. Friedan, *The Fountain of Age*, Vintage, 1994, p. 35.

exceptionally misleading; middle age, it has been stressed, was a
period of change but not necessarily of decline, a period of divergence much more than of convergence. These were the years, it must
be stressed, which saw improving health, declining mortality, rising
prosperity, new opportunities and growing expectations; these were
the years, it must now be accepted, which saw a growing divergence
in the health, prosperity, opportunities and aspirations of those in
their forties and fifties.

It has been suggested too that these differences depended less
upon individual choice and lifestyle than upon deep-seated, structural factors such as biology, genetic inheritence, gender identity
and class position. So while it was perfectly sensible for the middle
aged to try to live as healthily, behave as youthfully and think as positively as they could, it was – and is – unrealistic for those in their
forties and fifties to believe that they could thereby overcome all
the difficulties with which they found themselves confronted. For
as Marx remarked in a rather different context, men make their
own history, though not in the circumstances of their own choosing.[2]

It follows therefore that age is an important category for those
engaged in historical research. It remains, of course, exceptionally
difficult to steer between prescription and description, to distinguish between the characteristics that the middle aged possessed
because they were middle-aged and those that they possessed while
they were middle-aged.[3] Yet these difficulties must not be allowed
to disguise the necessity of bearing age divisions in mind. Age is a
category which should be placed alongside – and occasionally perhaps above – race, region, religion, gender and class when attempting to describe and explain the ways in which British people lived
and the ways in which British society developed during the course
of the twentieth century.

2. For example, M. Leier, *Red Flags and Red Tape: The Making of a Labour Bureau-
cracy*, University of Toronto Press, Toronto, 1995, p. 182.
3. T. K. Hareven, 'The Life Course and Ageing in Historical Perspective', in T. K.
Hareven and K. J. Adams (eds), *Ageing and Life Course Transitions: An Interdisciplinary
Perspective*, Tavistock, 1982, p. 3.

Appendix: The Wolverhampton Oral History Project

The interviews were carried out by Christopher Bennett and Steven Nicholls in late 1995 and early 1996.

Dr A. Aged 40 at time of interview (born 1955). West Midlands university lecturer. Separated, no children.

Mrs B. Aged 48 (born 1947). Owner, with her husband, of an East Midlands business centre. Married for 28 years, 25-year-old daughter lives nearby, 20-year-old son lives at home.

Mr C. Aged 41 (born 1954). Senior production manager in an East Midlands food production company. Married for 13 years (his second marriage) to Mrs D., 8-year-old daughter, 2-year-old son.

Mrs D. Aged 35 (born 1960). East Midlands child minder. Married for 13 years to Mr C., 8-year-old daughter, 2-year-old son.

Ms E. Aged 43 (born 1952). West Midlands university lecturer. Divorced while in her twenties, no children.

Mr F. Aged 49 (born 1947). Long-time West Midlands resident. Ex-teacher and trade-union official, dismissed at 47, now a full-time research student. Single.

Mr G. Aged 78 (born 1918). Ex-tailor and security guard in the Black Country. First wife died when he was in his forties, remarried when in his early sixties. 3 children with his first wife (one of whom died of cancer at age of 41), second wife has son of her own.

Mrs H. Aged 63 (born 1933). Lifelong Dudley resident. Former typist. Married for 40 years, 2 sons and a daughter in their thirties.

Mr I. Aged 75 (born 1921). Ex-owner of a building business in Staffordshire. Married Mrs I. when in his late thirties/early forties.

Mrs I. Aged 79 (born 1917). A war widow with one son, married Mr I. when in her late thirties/early forties. Helped Mr I. with his business accounts.

Mr J. Aged 87 (born 1908). Worked for 50 years as a coalminer in Cannock Chase. A widower with a 59-year-old son.

Mr K. Aged 79 (born 1917). A former West Midlands schoolteacher and local councillor. 2 children, one of whom is a university lecturer.

Mr L. Aged 48 (born 1947). Worked in Royal Navy, labouring, building, decorating and catering before taking undergraduate and postgraduate degrees in history. Unemployed and living on the South Coast. Unmarried.

Mr and Mrs M. Aged 70 (born 1925). Live in Staffordshire. Married with a 49-year-old son and 2 grandchildren.

Mr N. Aged 49 (born 1946). A Staffordshire postal worker. Married with 2 children.

Mrs O. Aged 60 (born 1935). Retired but serves as a magistrate in South Staffordshire. Married with 3 children and 4 grandchildren.

Mrs P. Aged 46 (born 1950). A senior probation officer. In the process of getting divorced, lives with her university lecturer partner in the West Midlands.

Mr Q. Aged 58 (born 1938). A former teacher and lifelong West Midlands resident. Wife a nurse, 1 daughter in her mid-20s who is studying abroad.

Index